How to Sit with God:
A Practical Guide
to Silent Prayer

How to Sit with
God

A Practical Guide
to Silent Prayer

Jean-Marie Gueullette
Translated by Kieran J. O'Mahony

VERITAS

Published 2018 by Veritas Publications
7–8 Lower Abbey Street
Dublin 1, Ireland
publications@veritas.ie
www.veritas.ie

ISBN 978 1 84730 838 2

10 9 8 7 6 5 4 3 2

A catalogue record for this book is available from the British
Library.

Cover designed by Heather Costello, Veritas Publications
Printed in the Republic of Ireland by SPRINT-print Ltd,
Dublin

*Veritas books are printed on paper made from the wood pulp of
managed forests. For every tree felled, at least one tree is planted,
thereby renewing natural resources.*

Contents

Introduction 7

Simple Prayer 13
All that is Required is an Act of Faith 50
Is it an Effective Form of Prayer? 68
How to Do It? 92
It is a Struggle and a Discipline 107
One Way of Praying Among Others 126
A Long History 143

Appendix 1: Biblical Texts for Silent Prayer 167
Appendix 2: Helpful Reading 176

Index of Authors 177

Introduction

Who are the intended readers of this book? Many paths may lead to a desire to know more about the Christian practice of silent prayer. Some – convinced Christians – having the desire to devote time to God each day, are not satisfied with their spiritual life. Perhaps a particular way of praying has nourished them for a time, but now they yearn for a renewal or a deepening of their relationship with God.

It could also be that received ideas about prayer cause dissatisfaction:

'A dialogue with God.' (But the common experience is to *hear* nothing.)

'A moment of intense relationship with the Lord.' (But each prayer session seems flooded by images, ideas or memories that have nothing to do with prayer.)

'Being still in the presence of God.' (But after a few minutes, many begin to feel uncomfortable and decide to end the session prematurely.)

These endlessly repeated expressions in spiritual literature or in preaching can lead to boredom, at best, and, at worst, to discouragement.

The Christian discourse on the spiritual life very often involves talk *about* prayer, but rarely a concrete teaching on *how* to go about it. It explores everything that prayer *could* be, without really taking into account the issues that most believers encounter, which are most often practical matters.

For this reason, others have – sometimes for many years – preferred to turn to meditation practices from Eastern traditions. Such people often have Christian roots, but paradoxically, it was their quest for God that took them away from the Church. They were in search of a practical teaching on prayer, silence, interiority and failed to find it in a Christian environment.

By contrast, non-Christian approaches met their needs: they offered an accessible practice, a way of doing things and a teaching on how to go about it; however, many Christians, after exploring these ways with honesty and perseverance for some time, find themselves gravitating again to their Christian faith. The silence, the discipline that they experience in yoga or Zen, paradoxically brings them back to the question of the place of Christ in their lives. Here again, it can be hard to find dialogue partners in the Church for people on such a pilgrimage. Some parishes and some priests welcome only with reluctance such spiritual pilgrims, highlighting the pitfalls that such practices may have for the Christian faith.

Nevertheless, in their spiritual life, this meditation experience developed outside the Church does not seem to the practitioner to have been a waste of time. It developed in them the ability to be present and enabled them to enjoy silence. Continuing their spiritual journey within a Christian framework may simply be a way of keeping this practice alive, but in more explicit reference to the presence of the living God. Having learned to be present, they can more easily understand what it means to be present *to God*.

In this book, we are offering to all, in the most practical sense possible, a very simple Christian way of praying in silence, while trying to refocus the time on the presence of God by the inner repetition of a name, the name of God.

This way of praying has a long history. There are some witnesses to it from the beginning of Christianity. It is so simple that it has no particular name. It has sometimes been called 'monologistic' prayer (prayer on a single word) or, more recently, 'centering prayer' or 'the prayer of simple regard'. At certain times, as demonstrated by the prevalence of German mysticism during the late medieval ages, for instance, it constituted a very popular way of praying. Today, much of this tradition in Christian heritage is completely ignored. This reinforces the idea that only Eastern traditions truly convey the importance of silence and interiority.

Without denying the richness of the contribution of the East in this regard, it is perhaps fruitful to listen to Christian spiritual teachers who have taught practices, including bodily and psychological approaches, which are consistent with the Gospel message and rooted in Western culture. The discovery of other traditions can be enriching, but it requires, if we are to be intellectually honest, quite an investment to understand the culture that gave rise to them in the first place.

The teaching of this Christian tradition is so simple that it can be received by all. It does not require any prior competence from a religious point of view, nor from a physical or psychological point of view. After several years of learning about silent prayer and teaching it to others, I am writing this book with the intention of bringing it to a wider audience.

Former students expressed the need for a text allowing them to return to 'this or that' aspect of the teaching, or to be able to meditate on one of the texts of the tradition. It was their request that prompted the writing of this book. But the witness given by people who have embarked on this spiritual adventure has also nourished that teaching in return. Different dimensions (one might even say 'tricks of the trade') have been discovered by different people in the creative fumbling which marks the spiritual life as it unfolds. Thanks is due to all for their trust, their creativity and their loyalty. Special thanks to Jean-Jacques Duchamp and Bob McKeon, companions from the very start. Bob's experience was a great benefit and he helped me organise the structure of this book. Such a mode of prayer, in its simplicity and sobriety, is not suitable for everyone. But experience shows that for those who find in it what they are looking for, it becomes the centre of gravity each day, the moment when they attune to the essential.

This approach is only one form of prayer among others. May the Spirit accompany everyone in their reading and in the concrete forms of putting into practice the quiet prayer suited to each individual.

Simple Prayer

THE APPEAL OF THE COMPLEX

The way of praying we are dealing with in this book is extremely simple and that is often the reason why it may seem difficult. We live complicated lives, constantly facing difficulties of all sorts. Simplicity does not come naturally to us, even in the spiritual life. If we feel that prayer life is not for us, we will tend to think that it is due to a lack of time and skill. 'If I do not pray, it's probably because it takes a lot of time, and anyway, I do not know how to do it.'

There is a story in the Bible that allows us to reflect on how we regard the relationship with God as something complicated, leading to the temptation to give it up (cf. 2 Kgs 5). Naaman the Syrian was a leper and he came to visit the prophet Elisha in the hope of being healed by him. Elisha gave him something very simple to do: to bathe seven times in succession in a river. Naaman was upset. He had hoped that the prophet would make an impressive gesture or utter mysterious words, and instead he told him take a bath! He began to sulk, saying that in his country one can take baths at any time and that it was really pointless to have travelled so far only to be offered such an obvious form of therapy.

His servant, wiser than his master, said to him, 'If the prophet had told you to do something extraordinary, would you not have done it?' Today, too, there is a growing interest in unusual therapeutic methods, using exotic substances or complicated exercises. Many are fascinated by intricate anthropological conceptions and are convinced that they have three bodies, or four, one of which is luminous, and so on. As such, it may seem quite glib to say that, in order to pray, all you need to do is take the right position and turn to the presence of God with your whole self. Still, this teaching is widely represented in the Christian tradition. Widely present and *yet ignored*, perhaps precisely because it is too simple!

GIVING ONESELF SIMPLY TO GOD

The Christian tradition places great importance on the mind in the spiritual life. By placing at the heart of its faith the reception of the Word of God, the tradition gives rise to an approach in which the word and our relationship to the written word are central. To listen to a word or to read a text requires not only that one seeks to understand, but also that one aspires to know the author. Thus, we are accustomed to using our intelligence in trying to know God, to understand his word and to understand ourselves. We know that such a quest is never over, but at least we have the feeling of knowing how to go about it. You have to read texts, think about them and possibly talk about them with others.

But to love God, how can this be done? How to love the one we do not see? There is a lot of talk of love in Christianity but does the love *of God* really have something to do with the various forms of human love? In asking such questions, we have gone back into *thinking*, and so we are no longer *loving*.

Our approach here is quite different. It is not really helpful to distinguish too much between knowing and loving, as if the effort to know God were an obstacle in having a relationship with him, or as if the love that a believer has for God had nothing to do with intellect, which is the very mark of a human being. When we oppose knowledge and love, it is very often because we put too much store in the act of knowing – for example, in the case of scientific knowledge – or that we put too much subjectivity in loving. But it is possible to combine the two interior movements, so that what we know of God nourishes the love that brings us to him and that this love brings him closer in a way that will help to discover God for what he really is.

All that is required is acts of love for God, with all our heart. All we need to do is love him with all our being, including our understanding, in a movement that includes adoration, veneration, trust, filial affection, friendship and hope. The essential thing is to give ourselves completely to him.

Why? Because it's the only way to get in touch with him on an equal footing. God gives himself totally to whoever welcomes him. He is present unconditionally, alongside those he has created and he looks on us as his children. All we can do is to give ourselves fully in return and keep ourselves present to him. What we need to remember is that the gift he makes of himself will always come before our response.

The human being is made in such a way that it is not possible for us to sustain the same interior activity for a long time. Soon, the worries of work and everyday preoccupations flood the mind and distract us from our movement towards God. Contemplative meditation is simply based on the division of time into small units; we are not able to love God and to give ourselves to him consistently over a long period, but we can do it in a succession of very short periods. At each of these moments, it is possible to want to love God and to want to be in his presence with all that we are.

THE PRAYER OF THE NAME

This way of praying is very simple: it consists of saying a word inwardly while sitting calmly. The prayer in this case is based on one word. The point is to take the name by which one spontaneously addresses God in prayer: *Father*, *Abba*, *Jesus*, *Lord*, *God*, *Kyrie eleison*, *Adonai* ... It is not necessary to pose many questions about the choice of this word. There is not one word that would be better than another or more effective. It is enough to take the name that one uses naturally and spontaneously for God. But it must be a name for God, not an idea about God or a description of God such as 'love' or 'goodness'.

In this way, the person praying engages their whole being in a movement of faith and love towards God, while they are pronouncing the name inwardly. Then it starts all over again. It's really no more complicated than that. The meaning of the word does not matter much, since one does not focus on it. We do not try to enjoy all the meanings and all the nuances. The essential thing is to turn to and rely on God by this name. As the *Catechism of the Catholic Church* says about the prayer on the name of Jesus, when repeated by a humbly attentive heart, 'the invocation of the holy name of Jesus is the simplest way of praying always' (*CCC*, 2668).

If we do not know which word to choose, we can pray to the Holy Spirit who prays in us and murmurs in our heart *Abba*, Father, as St Paul says (Rm 8:15–26). It is not complicated; it is enough to turn one's attention to God and let a name, by which we call on God, come spontaneously from the heart. Sometimes, one chooses initially, in an intellectual way, a word that seems right and full of meaning. Then, very quickly, after some time of prayer, another word suggests itself and replaces the first. Do not do this too often, but at the beginning, there is sometimes a brief period of adjustment.

Once one has begun to pray using that name, one continues with the same name, not only during the time prayer but also over a span of years. There is a notable difference between this and another form of similar repetitive contemplation, of which John Cassian already spoke in the fifth century. This consists of repeating throughout the day a verse or an expression which spoke to us upon reading the Bible or while praying the Psalms. This 'chewing the cud' approach is a way of prolonging reading in an almost physical way, of continuing to be nourished by a passage in the midst of other activities. This kind of reflection means we go on savouring the various meanings of a word or passage. For such activity, it is normal for us to change the word or phrase every day, the prayer resonating with daily readings. But in the prayer under discussion here, the name of God is not used to nourish reflection or to deepen some aspect of a mystery contemplated in the word. Its function is, rather, to be a point of support for staying in the presence of God, for holding our attention on God. When we have trouble walking, we do not change our walking stick at every outing! Likewise, we do not change the name we use.

Throughout life, silent prayer will be based on this same name. It has a simplifying effect: as soon as we say the name inwardly, we are in prayer, without having to ask ourselves questions about how we will go about it today. Mysteriously, this name becomes the path of interiority; it allows us to stand back and leave behind all the agitation by which we are distracted. It is difficult to explain, but all those who have experienced it will agree: the name allows us to have rapid access to a place of silence, this holy place that we carry within us, the sanctuary where God dwells. By means of this name, we know the way to this inner place.

THE NAME OF GOD

Though everyone has the freedom to use the word that is most natural to them, nevertheless we recommend using a word that is a name of God. To pronounce the name of someone is to refer to one person and not to another. To refer to what they are, but without defining that person. When we talk about someone using a nickname, a title or a psychological or professional moniker, we define the person more and we limit our point of view to our worldview or needs. If I go to see 'the doctor,' their emotional life or their taste for art does not concern me. I expect them to be a doctor and a good one at that. If someone is nicknamed 'Little Louis', it makes it very difficult to always keep in mind that Louis is great in other aspects of his person, even if he is limited in stature.

When we speak of God as 'the Saviour' or 'the Creator', what we say is true. But it correspondingly limits our perception of God. We choose an aspect of the mystery that touches us or that interests us, and we always risk believing that this aspect somehow contains the mystery and even says everything about God. Whereas if we say 'God', or 'Jesus', we are not concerned with what they do for us, but with who they are – which is always greater. When we say someone's name, we put ourselves in a relationship with that person, and at the same time, we say nothing about the individual and make no attempt to define the person. The knowledge we have of God is not of the order of definition or of description. An Orthodox monk of the late Middle Ages wrote:

> For when the mind unceasingly repeats the name of the Lord and the intellect gives its full attention to the invocation of the divine name, the light of the knowledge of God overshadows the entire soul like a luminous cloud. Concentrated mindfulness of God is followed by love and joy.[1]

How to Sit with God

Books of spirituality often refer to Jesus as 'my spouse' or 'my brother' or 'the good shepherd'. This is fine as far as it goes and does reflect part of the reality. But it runs the risk of limiting the relationship with God to one symbolic configuration, forgetting that the one of whom we speak is to be found beyond all such formulae. None of these is capable of saying who he is. There are different ways of overcoming the limited truth of such images. One approach would be to say all the possible names, as in litanies. Another approach would be to confine oneself to one name, which includes all the others because it does not single out a quality, an action or a role. Speaking the name of God places us in the presence of the one who is holy, greater than any human calculation. As St Peter Chrysologus taught in the fifth century with regard to the Lord's Prayer: 'We ask then that, just as the name of God is holy, so we may obtain his holiness in our souls.'[2]

To call on the name of the Lord: this is a very old definition of prayer, according to the verse of the prophet Joel, taken up by St Paul: 'Whoever calls on the name of the Lord will be saved' (Jl 3:5; Rm 10:13). To invoke the name of the Lord is to turn to him, to rely on him, without coming to him with any particular request. If salvation is linked to this invocation, is it not because the person locates themselves precisely as creature, incapable of saving themselves?

On the first of January, Francis de Sales sent a short letter to Jeanne de Chantal, before she went on to found the Visitation Order. While wishing her well, he encouraged her to repeat silently the name of God with love, so that God's presence would mark her whole life and her whole being:

> My daughter, I'm in such a hurry that I cannot write to you except to pass on the great word of our salvation: Jesus. Yes, my daughter, if only we could once say this holy name in our hearts. Oh, what a balm it would be to our whole spirit! May we be happy, my daughter, to have in mind only Jesus, in our memory only Jesus, in our will only Jesus, only Jesus in our imagination! Jesus would be everywhere in us and we would be everywhere in him. Let us try it, my dearest daughter, let us say it out loud. Often it will only be stammering but, in the end, we will be able to pronounce it well. But what is the benefit in saying, in pronouncing that sacred name? You have asked me to speak clearly. Alas, my daughter, I do not know! What I do know is that, in order to

express it well, one must have a tongue on fire, that is to say, it must be only through divine love and none other, thus, bringing Jesus to expression in our life, by imprinting him in the depths of our hearts. But have courage, my daughter, no doubt we will love God because he loves us. Be content and do not trouble your soul with anything else.[3]

LEAVE ASIDE WHATEVER IS NOT GOD

In saying this simple prayer word inwardly, the mind turns to God, as deeply as possible. It is difficult, if not impossible, to turn to God totally and without distraction for half an hour or an hour. Nevertheless, can we not engage as fully as possible, just for the time it takes to say a word? Then, we will just have to start all over again. Such a movement towards God requires two things: that we let go of all that concerns and distracts us and that we turn to God in faith. Dom Chapman, an English monk who lived in the early twentieth century, wrote: 'The simplest way of making an act of attention to God, is by an act of inattention to everything else.'[4]

This way of praying is indeed based on a movement of detachment from all that is not God. We must therefore detach ourselves from all worries, ideas and memories, whether good or bad. To detach oneself is not to reject or forget, but to leave things aside for a while, so as to be able to give oneself fully to God. We leave these things to one side so as to refocus on the presence of God. We can easily fill up our minds with holy thoughts and even loving our neighbour. These things are good in themselves; it is just that this is not the right moment for them.

If you try to be attentive to a friend who is confiding in you, you will be able to detach yourself from the noise of the street. In other circumstances, we might glance out the window. We will also let go of the memories, good or bad, that we have of our friend's previous visits, because they prevent us from receiving them as they are today. All sorts of ideas or images will cross our minds but we let them pass, in order to remain attentive to what our friend is telling us today. And this attention will not only be the concentration of the scientist focused on evidence, it will also be the declaration of the love living in us.

TURNING TO GOD, BODY AND SOUL

Our physical body can powerfully distract us and exclude us from our relationship with God; if we act as if the body did not exist, the body will soon remind us. If you sit awkwardly or in a position where it is difficult to breathe, you are not likely to be engaged in prayer for very long. The feeling of discomfort will make you want to shift, and each change of position will bring distraction, taking you back to the surface of the self. In other cases, you will not even think about moving, but the bodily discomfort will cause inner unease. Rather than draw the conclusion that you are not made for prayer, it is vital to learn some simple ways to enable sitting quietly. At any age, one may need to learn how to sit!

In the fourteenth century, an English hermit, Richard Rolle, emphasised the importance of sitting in contemplative prayer:

> As far as my study of Scripture goes, I have found that to love Christ above all else will involve three things: warmth, song and sweetness. And these three, as I know from personal experience, cannot exist for long without there being some quiet. If I were to stand up when I was engaged in contemplation or to walk about or even to lie prostrate on the ground I found that I failed to attain these three, and even seemed to be left in dryness. Consequently, if I were

to hold on to and retain deep devotion I must sit
— which is what I have decided to do. I am aware
that here is an underlying reason for this, for if a
man does much standing and walking his body gets
tired, and thus his soul too is hindered, wearied and
burdened. He is not as quiet as he can be and so is
not in his most perfect state; if the philosopher[5] is
right, it is the quiet sitting that makes the soul wise.
Let him who still stands more than he sits when
delighting in the things of God recognise that he has
a long way to go before he reaches the heights of
contemplation.[6]

AWAKE AND RELAXED, CONFIDENT AND RESPECTFUL
When we find ourselves at a meeting with Christians
and someone announces the moment for prayer, we
always see the participants shifting and changing
position. This is the expression of an intuition that
is often found in texts of the Christian tradition
that speak of the body in prayer: one does not hold
oneself just any way when one is consciously in the
presence of God. All our life is in the presence of God
and it is not because we are now attentive to him that
he suddenly becomes present to us. God is present
in our lives as he is present in the world as Creator.

He is present to us in a very special way because he made us his adopted children in Jesus Christ and he dwells in us through the Spirit, which has been poured into our hearts. These three modalities of God's presence are not evoked or transformed by our prayer. What changes is our attention to ourselves which, for a moment, we consciously bring into his presence. If we are turned towards him, we feel the need to adjust our body language. It is surely not a question of standing to attention, of becoming tense or striking strict and painful postures. Rather, by changing posture we signify that we are available. Our bodily attitude expresses our inner attitude and it also shapes it: the relationship between inner prayer and the body works both ways.

The goal is to find a way to be both attentive and relaxed. Prayer is not a relaxation exercise. If you fall asleep while praying, this may be a sign that you should spend more time sleeping at night, but it is also very likely that you are adopting a position which promotes drowsiness. It is mainly the spine that helps us stay awake: without being tense or stiff, it stands, resting on the pelvis, supported by our breathing. Thanks to the firmness of the back, the rest of the body is relaxed. We can compare this to a shirt placed on a clothes hanger that is held at arm's length: if the shirt can be fully unfurled, it is because we hold the hanger. The spine holds the hanger, that is the shoulders, and everything else is relaxed. In particular, attention must be paid to how one rests their shoulders. Often, tensions are concentrated there as a result of holding one shoulder higher than the other or pushing the shoulders forward. This causes pain in the upper back. There is nothing to do but to let the shoulders fall, like the shirt on the hanger: nothing more complicated.

THERE IS A RIGHT POSTURE FOR EVERYONE

There can be no question of defining the posture of silent prayer, of proposing a single way of sitting which is essential for this practice. Each one of us is built differently and one way of being still that will be good for one person will cause pain in the other. One can draw inspiration from a neighbour's way of doing things, as long as it proves to be effective. It is important not to be overwhelmed by the example of others, leading perhaps to unsuitable postures. Everyone needs to find their own way of sitting. This may require adjustments over a long period, to find the right seat height, a good position for the hands and so on. Do not be afraid to experiment or try different solutions.

Ignoring feelings of pain or standing still can be physically harmful and may not lend itself to prayer. If we ignore what our body is telling us, it will soon become our main concern.

Whatever solutions we come across, in order to be able to sit for half an hour, the key is not to move and not to even think of moving. One does not put oneself under constraint, under the weight of which one would merely endure the time of meditation while sighing and suffering, waiting for deliverance.

Although there are various ways of sitting, such as on a small bench or on a cushion, there is nevertheless an anatomical constant, applicable in all circumstances: the manner of positioning one's pelvis. The deepening of the spiritual life can include very concrete aspects and the following little exercise allows us to understand this essential and basic point.

Sit in the middle of a chair and let yourself go back with your back against the backrest. Notice how your pelvis is in contact with the chair and take note of its point of support. Note that your back, leaning against the back of the chair, is curved. Without moving the point of support of the pelvis, move your head forward, which will gradually bring your back forward. At some point, as you lean forward, your centre of gravity on the chair will tip forward. The part of the pelvis on which you sit is not a single point, but a two-pointed bone, which allows two possible positions of the pelvis with respect to the chair.

In meditation, you have to sit in the position where the pelvis is tilted forwards, not backwards. This means that the upper thighs are well placed on the chair and that, in most cases, the knees are lower than the pelvis.

Small prayer stools, in which the upper board is slightly inclined forwards, oblige the pelvis to take this position. Once you have understood these two positions, you can sit at the edge of the chair, the pelvis forward, so that you do not feel the need to lean on the back of the chair. This positioning of the pelvis has two important effects: on the one hand, it places the back in a stable and natural position; on the other, it frees the abdomen to breathe properly. With the pelvis forward, the lower back has a slight curve, which is natural to it. Also, if one leans on a vertical plane, like a wall, one must feel two points of contact, at the level of the sacrum and the shoulders, the rest of the back being taken off the wall. This curvature is normal and it would be detrimental to oblige oneself to press the whole back to the wall to 'stand straight'. One would stand upright, but at the cost of damaging the natural mechanisms that allow us to stand up straight.

If you meditate on a chair, once the pelvis is in place with the upper thighs resting well on the whole chair, what about the feet? If the height of the chair allows it, they are laid flat on the floor, a little apart. If the chair is too low, leave the legs loose under the chair, possibly crossing them, keeping the thighs firmly placed on the chair. This suggests that for everyone, there is a chair height that is optimal, and that is not necessarily the standard height. Try various chairs that are available to you, and if you do not find one that allows you to sit comfortably while having your feet flat on the floor, do not hesitate to choose a lower or higher chair or to add a cushion.

A young woman came to see me one day to tell me about her difficulties in prayer. As I asked her, 'How do you pray?' she answered me with very spiritual words about prayer, emphasising her personal mediocrity. As I repeated my question, she finally heard me, a smile appeared on her face and she said to me: 'In fact, I think my little red chair is too low ...' Finally taking the time to think about her practice then in a truly practical way, she at last recognised that the position did not suit her, and admitted that she had never thought of changing it. Could a change in the way we sit be part of the way of prayer?

You may feel the need to sit on the floor. It is not so much to 'feel energy from the ground', as we sometimes hear, but to seek greater stability. When sitting on a chair, even if you take the trouble to sit properly, the support surfaces on which the weight of the body rests are limited and one always feels a little 'on stilts'. There are many ways to sit on the floor; some require learning so as to acquire gradually the necessary flexibility.

If you are meditating on a prayer stool, check that it is tilted and that the height is right for you. You can increase its height, if necessary, by placing small wedges under the feet of the stool or by putting a cushion on the stool. If after a few minutes you get cramps or pins and needles in the calves, find another solution and do not force it. Do not hesitate to put a rug or blanket under your knees to make the ground less hard in support of the knees. If this form of sitting suits you, you will see that it has the advantage of placing the back in a comfortable position, straight without being stretched, and that it facilitates not moving. If you widen your knees a little, in a triangle, you will notice an improvement in both steadiness and deep breathing from the abdomen.

If one meditates on a cushion, it must be sufficiently firm and high (10 to 20 cm). Another possibility would be to use folded blankets. Avoid sitting on a foam or feather pillow as it will be too soft and will not provide sufficient height. One can adopt the cross-legged position like the half-lotus or the full lotus.

Sitting cross-legged will not be easy if you try it directly on the floor. It requires a cushion or folded blanket. Otherwise, one of the disadvantages of this position, which is accessible to almost everyone, is to tilt the pelvis backwards. The back will then be struggling to straighten. The situation improves somewhat if one sits on a good cushion. Leaning against a wall can also help. The other problem is that the surfaces of contact with the ground are slender. The weight of the legs rest only on the heels. The feet rest themselves on the ground by the outer edge. This does not induce a feeling of great stability. This can be remedied by placing small cushions between the knees and the floor, outside of the feet: this increases the contact surface and helps the legs to relax.

If you feel good cross-legged on a cushion, you can uncross your legs on the ground. This posture is known as the diamond. Sometimes we do it more easily on one side than on the other. One can gain flexibility by placing a cushion temporarily under the less flexible leg. This way one will relax, thanks to the cushion, and, little by little, by repeating the exercise for a few days or a few weeks, it will become possible to put both legs on the ground. When it works, this posture is good for the back and allows you to sit well. It can irritate some, because the angle of the knee is quite sharp. It is better not to practise it with tight trousers on since they may interfere with the circulation of the blood.

The half-lotus and lotus positions provide the greatest stability, at the cost of closing the knees a little. These last two postures, very suitable for meditation, must be learned only very gradually, in order to avoid hurting the joints.

It is particularly dangerous to try to reach the half-lotus by taking one's leg and placing it on the other knee with the hands, forcing it a little. It is generally only after long practice that one can acquire the necessary suppleness for the half-lotus or the full lotus, a suppleness which comes from elsewhere in the joint of the hip, and not from the knee. These postures are not suitable for everyone, so they should never be forced. The complete lotus has the advantage of giving a perfectly stable and symmetrical posture, since both knees rest on the ground and the back is placed just right. It is a position that lends itself to meditation because it supports the back and facilitates relaxation in the rest of the body.

The practice of these two postures requires patient relaxation work, the half-lotus being more accessible than the full lotus. It is best to learn under the guidance of someone competent, for example, as part of a yoga class.

RELAXED BREATHING

When sitting in a proper posture, the breathing calms down naturally and gradually. You do not breathe with your shoulders like when you need air after running. On the contrary, the breathing is governed by the abdomen, which fills out when we breathe in. If you are unfamiliar with this feeling, you can practise outside of prayer time by putting your hand flat on your belly to feel this movement and also to foster it.

In the gentle breathing that comes with bodily repose, only breathing out is an effort. We do not need to look for air, we just have to empty the air inside us. In fact, the muscles that lie between the ribs have the function of reducing the volume of the ribcage, bringing the ribs closer together. Like springs, they let the ribs spread as soon as they are no longer contracted, and this movement allows the ribcage to fill with air. Again, if you are unfamiliar with this, take a little time to observe what's going on. Notice that if you exhale completely, you just have to let go, to stop exhaling so that breathing in takes place spontaneously.

It does not seem necessary during prayer to pay too much attention to these phenomena. It is good to know about them and then to let them just happen. Breathing exercises can be helpful and beneficial, but they should not interfere with the time devoted to prayer. Our main concern is the presence of God and not our own breathing. We will come back to this because when one finds oneself beset with worries or emotions that distract us from prayer, becoming aware of one's breathing by taking deep breaths can be a good way to get back on track and to keep oneself in the 'here and now'.

THE BODY AND CHRISTIAN PRAYER

If, in contrast to other religions, Christian spiritual teachers have said very little about precise bodily methods regarding prayer, it was not because of ignorance on their part or because of contempt for the body. They were convinced that it is an integral part of the human person and therefore also of the praying person. But they were also convinced that the correct bodily posture is secondary. Thus, they generally preferred to consider positions of the body as an expression of the state of the soul, rather than risking the development of methods which would have suggested a power of the body over the soul or even the power of a technique over God. Attention to the body is important, but it is a secondary consideration. For example, how can you claim to know rest in God if you cannot stop fidgeting? This was the question asked in the seventeenth century by Fr Guilloré, a Breton Jesuit:

Be honest, do not you often change your position at prayer, preoccupied with the postures you take, thinking only of easing the body and trying to be comfortable and attain a kind of gentle indolence? You know that this is almost the sum total of what you do in prayer and that almost every body part in is motion.

After that, you fool yourself into thinking your prayer is only what you think of it. Learn that this simple prayer, which brings together everything into one, itself looks after the body and communicates to it what it communicates to the mind. It gives the mind inner stillness by the gentleness of its repose and communicates also to the body something of this peaceful consistency.[7]

If you want to prevent the head, arms and legs from moving constantly, you have to start thinking about them a bit. If you want to avoid thinking about your bodily discomfort, it is best to pay attention to how one sits. Here we find a constant of spiritual life: we cannot really acquire freedom, detach ourselves, except from what we know, from what we have identified. If we ignore our body, head, arms and legs, we will not be able to be still!

For those who arrive at the moment of prayer, feeling especially nervous and the prospect of staying motionless seems too difficult, it is possible to begin with a time of preparation, so to speak, during which one walks as slowly as possible in the room, being attentive to the sensations and the unevenness caused by walking. Hands placed flat on the stomach or chest may help you to become aware of your breathing. If time and space permit doing this outdoors, it can be very relaxing. Such a practice induces an inner calmness and makes one more open to prayer. This works very well if you wish to join two silent prayer periods: a few minutes of such a meditative walk allow one to stretch without going out of the inner space, which is prayer.

IS THIS A TECHNIQUE?

Such practical indications may surprise or even worry some people. We are more accustomed to hearing speeches about prayer than to receiving practical instruction on how to do it. But that's what we probably need most. It is not difficult to be convinced of the necessity of prayer, but very often, this conviction is undermined by practical difficulties that we do not dare to speak of and that we quickly interpret as mediocrity or failure. Instead of recognising that we really do not know how to keep quiet, we are going to invent a whole speech to convince ourselves that we are not a contemplative or that we are great sinners, whose faults have destroyed the ability to pray. It is easier to say that one is not mystical, than to recognise that one is ill at ease.

A TECHNIQUE TO MANIPULATE GOD?

A question often comes up when one considers such practical details: are we not, by such means, setting up psychological processes instead of praying? Can the grace of God be confined to techniques? This is a good question, because it clarifies the respective roles of creator and creature in prayer. God gives unconditionally; therefore, it cannot be triggered by human practices. It is not a reward granted to those who correctly implement this or that method! But it is a gift that respects human freedom. That is to say, it does not impose itself and it does not transform me if I refuse the gift. The responsibility of the human being is not to *earn* the gift of God, but simply to *welcome* it. If the gift of God is not received, if God is not welcomed, God will not be effective. So it is with contemplative prayer. Its methods do not have the effect of making God present. God is present, whatever happens on our side. But we are not present and we are always somewhere else. If we look at our distractions in prayer, we quickly realise that these are always ideas, sensations or emotions that bring us elsewhere. We think about what we have done, or what we should have done, or what we still have to do. In short, we are somewhere else.

When they were teaching prayer, the spiritual masters of the Christian tradition also looked for ways to be present and available to the presence of God. These means cannot really be felt because they are merely means. This is probably why Christian texts on the practical forms of prayer are relatively restrained. They give indications, but most often leave a great deal of freedom for everyone to find the solutions that suit each one. For example, you can find in the Desert Fathers (third to fourth century) traces of teaching on posture. They insist on the importance of sitting, to the point of making it an equivalent of prayer or even of monastic life, that some define as 'sitting down in one's cell'. But they give the bare minimum of details about how to sit down, as if they were telling each other to do their own 'research' in this area. A little later, we find in

St Augustine the same caution with regard to any prescription of a posture for prayer:

> Nothing is prescribed in regard to the attitude which the body must keep in order to pray, provided that the soul, attentive to God, expresses its desires. We can indeed pray standing, as it is written, 'The publican stood at a distance' (Lk 18:13). We can also pray on our knees, as we read in the Acts of the Apostles (Acts 7:59, 20, 36); or sit, like David and Elijah. Finally, if we could not pray while even lying down, it would not have been recorded in the Psalms: 'Every night, I will bathe my bed of tears, I will sprinkle my bed with my tears' (Ps 6,7). When in fact one prepares to pray, each one takes the most appropriate bodily position according to the state of one's soul.[8]

There is no bodily attitude that is prescribed as being most favourable to Christian prayer. On the other hand, Christian spiritual teachers commit the believer to finding, according to one's physical condition, culture and location, an attitude that is conducive to prayer. Not teaching a specific posture does not mean that all positions are equal. Everyone must adopt a proper posture, that is to say, a posture that is appropriate, not only in terms of personal comfort, but that is appropriate for prayer. In this way, the posture expresses one's desire to seek to live in the presence of God. Such integration has a cultural dimension: some gestures or postures may be suitable for prayer in one culture and may be considered unsuitable or inappropriate in another.

Such Christian flexibility should not be regarded as a sign of ignorance or contempt for bodily or psychological realities, but as a way of leaving such things in their place, which is not at the centre. It must be admitted that in more recent times, this secondary place has been devalued to the point where there has been no practical handing on of it in prayer. We have been able to transmit and learn texts and prayers, but by addressing almost exclusively the intellect. This is certainly one of the reasons that drove so many Christians to Eastern practices: they sought in other cultures what the Christian community no longer handed on, even though it really was part of the tradition.

THE MEANS CHANGE WITHOUT CHANGING GOD

For this way of praying, centred as it is on the presence of God and our presence to God, the big challenge is precisely *being there*. 'God is always ready, but we are unready; God is near us, but we are far from him; God is in but we are out; God is at home (in us), but we are abroad,' said Meister Eckhart.[9] We are outside, strangers, unstable, and these practical ways help us to refocus on the presence of God. Father Thomas Keating, a contemporary American Trappist monk,[10] calls this way of praying 'centering prayer' which draws attention to the never finished task of becoming one with God. It is not a question of going on a journey towards God, but of refocusing oneself by means of prayer. In this centre, in the depths of our soul, we can hold ourselves in his presence.

The methods under discussion here act upon us and not upon God. No respiratory or bodily technique has any effect on God and it is not because I can meditate upside down that he will be more attentive to me! On the other hand, the practical means are there to make us more available and to help us to be present. We can therefore speak of techniques in prayer, as long as we remember that we are the ones undergoing change.

How to Sit with God

Christian theology is always careful to reject any spiritual teaching which suggests that salvation can be the fruit of our own efforts: union with God and salvation are given by him, without earning or meriting on our part. The notion of gift is central to the Christian conception of the relationship to God. On our own, we cannot make this relationship happen. We can only make ourselves available to the gift coming from God. Such availability is indeed spiritual, but within an incarnate religion, it would be utterly incoherent to hold that the spiritual can develop apart from the body and without relation to it. Bodily techniques are not a substitute for the gift of God, but they help the one who prays to be more attentive and open.

TECHNIQUES HARMFUL TO THE FAITH?

If these techniques have an effect only on us, and not on God, does this make it possible to integrate into Christian prayer methods developed in other cultural and religious systems? Is there no risk involved in sitting in a lotus position for prayer when one is a Christian? For example, a question often asked of Christians who practise yoga, who even integrate this practice into their prayer, is that of implied adherence to another religious system. It would indeed be very reductive to make yoga a simple body technique, a hip kind of gymnastics. Yoga was born in a very particular culture and religious context. It is consistent with a worldview and with an understanding of what it is to be human and what our relationship with the transcendent might be. By practising yoga, do we not thereby risk becoming part of this system and risk abandoning the Christian vision?

The question has its share of truth and it must remain present in the minds of Christians who have taken up such practices. However, it must not lead us to forget that the body, and what we do with the body, lacks meaning when viewed apart from a language and culture. To prostrate one's forehead to the ground does not mean that one is necessarily engaged in an act of Muslim worship, any more than the lotus position entails an unavoidable adherence to Buddhism. The Christian can therefore take advantage of the wisdom of the bodily experience of the East, knowing how to draw from it what can help in terms of Christian practice. On the other hand, certain Buddhist practices (for example, exploring impermanence so that the subject is dissolved into the cosmos) cannot be engaged in without undermining Christian faith, which is based on the personal relationship with God who discloses himself by his Word.

The Church Fathers and medieval theologians were able to borrow from the Greek, Jewish and Arab philosophers whatever concepts they needed, without, at the same time, espousing all their conclusions. In the same way today, Christians can go to the school of Eastern bodily wisdom while remaining rooted in their faith, which will lead them to avoid certain practices or theories. They will then also be able to engage with those who undertake the same practices, albeit with another religious worldview.

The question that faith puts to Eastern bodily practices ultimately goes back to the eternal problem of being Christian: how can we, in a complex world, hold on to whatever is good, ask meaningful questions, and dare to take risks? Just because things *may* go wrong is no reason not to take paths potentially fruitful for the faith.

NOTES

1. Theoleptos of Philadelphia, †1320 'On Inner Work in Christ and the Monastic Profession': G.E.H. Palmer, Philip Sherrard, Kallistos Ware (eds), The *Philokalia: The Complete Text,* Volume IV, London: Faber and Faber, 1995, p. 181.

2. Peter Chrysologus, *Sermon* 71, cited in the *Catechism of the Catholic Church*, §2814.

3. St Francis de Sales, letter 628 to the Baroness de Chantal, 1 January 1608. English version by the translator.

4. John Chapman, *Spiritual Letters*, London: Continuum, 2003, Letter XLIII (Letter 5), p. 122.

5. Rolle means Aristotle.

6. Richard Rolle, *The Fire of Love,* translated into modern English by Clifton Wolters; London: Penguin Books, 1972; Chapter 14, p. 89.

7. *Conférences spirituelles pour bien mourir à soi-même* par le R.P. François Guilloré tome premier, à Paris, chez Étienne Michallet, premier imprimeur du Roy, rue S. Jacques à l'image S. Paul près la fontaine S. Séverin, MDCLXXXIX, p. 337. English version by the translator.

8. Saint Augustine, 'Quelle attitude adopter dans la prière?', Questions à Simplicianus, l. II, q. IV, Bibliothèque augustinienne 10, trad. Gustave Bardy, p. 569–571. English version by the translator.

9. Meister Eckhart, *Sermons & Treatises,* Volume II, translated and edited by M. O'C. Walshe; Longmead: Element Books, 1979; Sermon 69, p. 169.

10. Thomas Keating, *Open Mind, Open Heart: The Contemplative Dimension of the Gospel*, New York: Continuum, 1992.

All that is Required is an Act of Faith

THE PRESENCE OF GOD IN US

One of the great Christian contributions is the affirmation of God's presence in the soul. The holy place *par excellence* is no longer the temple but deep within the soul, where, according to the words of Jesus to the Samaritan woman, 'true worshippers worship the Father in spirit and in truth.' There is therefore no holy place, properly speaking in Christianity, where God dwells specifically. A sixth-century Greek Christian expressed this in a pithy manner: 'You are a temple, do not look for a place.'[1]

AN ACT OF FAITH

The Christian tradition recognises the presence of God in every creature, for he is the author of all and keeps everything in being. It recognises the presence of Christ in the community, gathered in his name, in the service of the poor and in the sacraments. It also recognises the presence of God in the soul for two reasons. First, because God created it in his image and as a result, God is at home there. Second, because the incarnation has made the depth of the soul (the mark of our human nature which distinguishes us from all other living beings) the place of our union with Christ.

JOHN AND PAUL: WITNESSES TO GOD'S PRESENCE

In the New Testament, we find affirmations that support this way of looking at things. John's meditation on the disciple's relationship with the Lord is enriched by the notion of inner dwelling: 'Those who love me will keep my word, and my Father will love them, and we will come to them and make our home with them' (Jn 14:23). In the same way, the metaphor of the union of the branches with the vine includes this injunction: 'Abide in me as I abide in you' (Jn 15:4). Other passages from the Farewell Discourse (Jn 14–17) teach the same.

From his personal experience Paul summarises with the formula: 'It is no longer I who live, but it is Christ who lives in me' (Gal 2:20). Saint Paul also developed the idea that we are the temple of the Holy Spirit: 'Do you not know that you are God's temple and that God's Spirit dwells in you?' (1 Cor 3:16). He spells out the consequences in two areas of life: prayer and morality. In his teaching on prayer, Paul invites his readers to recognise that this relationship with God, this word addressed to God, is possible only if the Spirit of the Lord brings it alive in us. This is the same Spirit that Paul says makes us adopted children and through whom we cry out 'Abba, Father' (Rm 8:15). 'Likewise the Spirit', continues Paul a little further, 'helps us in our weakness; for we do not know how to pray as we ought, but that very Spirit intercedes with sighs too deep for words' (Rm 8:26).

This teaching on the presence of the Holy Spirit in us is not limited to the spiritual life. It has, in Paul's eyes, very practical consequences for our behaviour. The body is the temple of God and so it cannot be used for immorality and idolatry. 'Your body is a temple of the Holy Spirit within you, which you have from God. Therefore, glorify God in your body' (1 Cor 6:19–20).

Learning, in quiet prayer, to recognise this presence of God within us is not an easy process, for if we stay with it, it will eventually involve our whole being – and not only during times of prayer – which is now lived in the presence of God. Certain kinds of behaviour gradually seem weird or even absurd for the person who sees this presence of God in our bodily existence. Why do so many Catholics show a profound respect for the presence of God in the Eucharist and yet evidently dishonour themselves in their bodies and emotional lives?

OUR RESPONSIBILITY

This is how Meister Eckhart spoke of this presence, commenting on the Gospel story of the buyers and sellers being thrown out of the Temple:

> This temple, in which God would rule with authority, according to his will, is man's soul, which he has made exactly like himself, just as we read that the Lord said: 'Let us make man in our image and likeness' (Gn 1:26). And this he did. So, like himself has God made man so that nothing else in heaven or on earth, of all the splendid creatures that God has so joyously created, resembles God so much as the human soul. For this reason, God wants this temple cleared, that he may be there all alone. This is because this temple is so agreeable to him, because it is so like him and he is so comfortable in this temple when he alone is there.[2]

How to Sit with God

It is our responsibility to ensure that the soul is free and available for God to take up residence there. Meister Eckhart knew well that many ideas, images, projects or painful memories can occupy all the space in us, to the point where there is no place for God:

> Now all God wants of you is for you to go out of yourself in the way of creatureliness and let God be within you. The least creaturely image that takes shape in you is as big as God. How is that? It deprives you of the whole of God. As soon as this image comes in, God has to leave with all his Godhead. But when the image goes out, God comes in. God desires you to go out of yourself (as creature) as much as if all his blessedness depended on it. My dear friend, what harm can it do you to do God the favour of letting him be God in you? Go right out of yourself for God's sake, and God will go right out of *himself* for your sake![3]

As soon as a thought enters this holy place within, God is excluded, because I cannot attend to two realities at once and I cannot commit my will in two directions at the same time. The time of silent prayer is the moment *par excellence* when I must let God be God in me, letting him occupy that space within. To enter, to go out, to take up space: all these are images, to try to express the presence of God, but these images are very telling, because we know how much we can be completely invaded by a project, by a love experience, by an inner struggle. Today, when young people say that something 'does my head in', they express well this impression that their whole being is taken over, invaded by a concern, some image or picture. Silent prayer is the moment when these images must be cleared out, when nothing but God must occupy the centre of the soul. On the surface, these things don't bother us because we are always immersed in the noise of the world. The problems which occupy us still remain present, on the surface, but we deny them access, at least for a while, to our inner self. We struggle – and sometimes it is hard work – to ensure that such thoughts do not take the place which belongs to God, in the inner temple of the soul.

A TWO-WAY PRESENCE

As with the other ideas or images we use to express our relationship with God, the language of presence is fine but it does not capture the whole mystery. In particular, it should be possible to say that 'to dwell in' – what theology calls indwelling – is reciprocal between God and the human person. God is always in us, but we are called to abide in God. The Confessions of St Augustine begin with this famous phrase: 'You have made us for yourself, O Lord, and our heart is restless until it comes to rest in you.' A deep human relationship, of love or friendship, can give an idea of this kind of reciprocity. A person may have the feeling of carrying within themselves the presence of the friend, who accompanies her in all things, even if he is at the other end of the world or perhaps even dead. The security that one feels from the presence of the other is not destroyed by physical absence.

This works two ways. Sometimes, we can be very moved to discover that we are precious in the eyes of a person who is precious in our own eyes. Each carries within the presence of the other. The Gospel of John offers a very particular application of this experience to the relationship with Jesus and it can be read as an echo of the friendship between Jesus and the beloved disciple in that Gospel.

Awareness of this reciprocity of presence between God and us protects us from a potential risk in contemplating the presence of God, a risk of reducing God to the confines of my own life, a little 'portable

God', so to speak. To say that God is present in the human heart is not to lose sight of his grandeur. Augustine attempts to express this paradox in the Confessions (III, 6), when he acknowledges in the same sentence that God is closer to him than he is to himself and still always greater than even the most sublime human thought.

Once more, reflection on the mystery has practical consequences: if I am as conscious as possible that God, whose presence in me I acknowledge by faith, is also the Almighty and the creator of the universe, this must lead to an attitude of deep respect, which then translates into a bodily attitude. God's presence cannot be treated simply as a comfort when life is difficult and then ignored when all is well.

ATTENDING TO THE PRESENCE OF GOD

Meditation on this mysterious presence of God within has long led Christians to recognise a certain paradox, a painful experience brought about by silent prayer. It is not a question of generating God within or even of approaching God. It is a question of recognising in faith that God is present in me, but that during this time, I am completely facing outwards, fascinated by the joys and sorrows of the world. The difficulty is not finding God, since he is already within us, but attending fully to that presence; therefore, there is a close link between the capacity for interiority (presence to oneself) and prayer (presence to God).

The path of Christian interiority does not have as its first purpose introspection or self-knowledge, but the quest for God, in the holy place where he resides, that is, in the depths of our humanity. William de Saint-Thierry, a twelfth-century monk, close to St Bernard, prayed thus:

> As long as I am with you, I am also with me: on the other hand, I am not with me as long as I am not with you. And woe to me, every time I'm not with you, without whom I cannot even exist.[4]

Prayer is therefore a tireless movement of coming back to yourself, in which the believer catches himself moving outwards so as to focus his attention again and therefore his own self-awareness, where God is waiting for him.

AN ACT OF FAITH IN THE PRESENCE OF GOD

This presence of God within cannot be felt. It is not because one feels a warmth in the chest that can detect the presence: why would God be hot or cold? The one who prays does not seek to feel the presence of God, but rather is called upon to believe in it. As we refocus the mind, directing our meandering thoughts on the presence of God, we fix our will and loving attention on this presence and focus on it through an act of faith. Through the entire prayer time, we hold this attitude of faith. At each inward saying of the name, we turn to the one we name and believe to be present and we attach ourselves to God with all our heart. Thus, one orthodox monk of the fourteenth century teaches:

> Sitting in your cell, then, be mindful of God, raising your intellect above all things and prostrating it wordlessly before him, exposing your heart's state to him, and cleaving to him in love.[5]

Speaking of the will might seem to evoke a strained attitude. But that would be to forget that to want is to desire freely, to choose to desire so to speak. The question during prayer is therefore, 'What do I choose as the object of my desire, to what am I drawn with all my being?' It is important that we are clear about the object of our desire and do not bestow our desire on anything less worthy. Dom Chapman wrote:

> We want to use our will to 'want God', and not to keep our thoughts in order. We want to be 'wanting God', and detached from everything else. Hence we *want* to let our thoughts run about by themselves (I think you will recognise what this means) and not to control them; in order that our will may turn wholly to God. The result is naturally that, while our will is making its intense (but almost imperceptible) act of love, our imagination is running about by itself, just as it does in a dream; so that we *seem* to be full of distractions, and not praying at all. But this is the contrary of the fact. The distractions, which are so vivid to us, are not *voluntary* actions, and have no importance; whereas the *voluntary* action we are performing is the *wanting* God, or giving ourselves to God.[6]

A SABBATH FOR GOD

Silent prayer is an activity marked by this intense act of the will, by an act of faith tirelessly made new in the presence of God. At the same time, it is a question of doing nothing in the presence of God. It is not a time of relaxation or pure passivity, but all external activity is suspended so that the attention is wholly directed to the act of faith. Any external activity is set aside: not only work, productivity, or talk, but also all unnecessary worry.

THE SABBATH: A CHANCE TO BE FREE

The Sabbath was instituted in Israel when the people had come out of Egypt: they had to be freed from slavery in order to stop working. Once a week, on the Sabbath, the people of God stopped working: it is the Sabbath for the Lord, a time when no work is done. And this is more than a healthy habit; it is a rhythm providing necessary rest. The Sabbath is an opportunity to remember that one is no longer a slave, that one has the possibility of not working, because the meaning of a human life cannot be based exclusively on work. In the presence of God, it is not by our work that we exist, but because we are loved by our creator. It is very beneficial to consider the time of silent prayer in this way, as a miniature Sabbath each day. During the time of prayer, all work stops, and it is good to ensure that the work does not invade the prayer. So many hyperactive Christians spend the time of their prayer asking God for forgiveness for what they did not do, as well as for his strength to do more, asking God to put himself to work too. Such prayer of petition is God's 'to do' list! They themselves exist only by their activity and naturally, they think that God must be in the same category.

Silent prayer introduces a break in this hellish spiral of work and efficiency. Silent prayer is 'useless', that is, not useful and must remain a time of freedom. If too much attention is paid to the method, with an exaggerated concern to do well, transforming this time for God into a moment of effort, along with the temptation to evaluate its quality, then we have gone completely astray. If you lead a very active lifestyle and feel there are never enough hours in the day, you are the ideal candidate for silent prayer. Silent prayer is not reserved for the sick or retired, or those with ample free time. A busy day will be transformed if it is punctuated by a period of thanksgiving, a Sabbath for the Lord.

SALVATION IS NOT BY WORKS

Often, after a few months or a few years of silent prayer, people who are engaged in a very active life note that their relationship to activity has evolved.

They work no less than before, but they do not do it any longer in exactly the same way. There is indeed a way of working that is related to the fact that we are, more or less consciously, convinced that salvation is found in work: the more I work, the more I am recognised, the more I exist. And when the amount of work becomes overwhelming, a revealing expression appears: 'I'll never be done ...' Be done, as if I were absolutely alone and the exit, salvation, could come only from me.

With such convictions, it is obvious that one will fail, given the magnitude of the task. But if each workday is marked by a time spent precisely *not* working, free in the presence of God, many things can change. Many people point out that this time seems to them more and more like the centre of gravity of their day, the truest, the most 'right' moment, in relation to which all activity is ordered, and put back into its proper place. To spend time freely in the presence of him whom by faith I recognise as my saviour, to stand before the one of whom I know, in whose eyes I know, in faith, that I am precious whatever I do, that puts all work into perspective. In the presence of God, it is not by my work, by my efficiency or even by my successes that I exist, but because *I am myself* and God created me. To become aware of this basic identity every day in silent prayer does not trigger laziness, and does not cause anyone to stop being active. Instead, all note that they no longer work in the same way and that they gradually acquire a certain interior detachment which enables them to avoid being overwhelmed or even made unwell by work.

SILENT PRAYER: A SUCCESSION OF ACTS OF THE WILL
In 1925, Dom Chapman wrote to a nun:

> But when we pass on to 'Contemplative Prayer'
> … we seem to be idle, mooning, wasting time. But though we cannot feel that we are active, we perceive, when we reflect upon it, that we are *intensely* active. To *sit and want God intensely* is obviously an intense act of the will. In order to concentrate on this intense act, we want to stop all other action.[7]

'To sit down and want God intensely' are two acts of the will by which this monk perfectly sums up contemplative prayer. When our days are already too full, we wake wondering if we will be able to 'get everything done' by the evening; we know only too well that it takes a great will power to make time to sit down for God. And we see here that the fact that silent prayer is practised sitting is of great importance.

One can, of course, pray while walking, while travelling and the Rosary lends itself very well to such a practice. But such practice does run the risk of not spending time explicitly with God. We consecrate a part of ourselves, while we do something else. What would you think if a friend, when you want to talk to her about something that worries you, replies, 'No problem, I'm listening, but we're going to talk while walking, because I have to do shopping, go to the post office, and visit a sick person. But come with me, we'll have plenty of time to talk on the way.' It's likely that you would find it very difficult to speak candidly under such circumstances. There is an availability that requires us to stop and a quality of mutual presence that we can only know by taking the time to sit down. Very often, in Europe, we use the expression 'we need to talk', whereas Africans would say, 'We need to sit down.' So this is the first decision, and not always the easiest: to sit for God.

The second act of the will, described by Dom Chapman, is to desire God intensely. This is what is going to occupy us during the time of contemplative prayer: to do nothing, except to bring one's desire and will to God, relying on his name. It is therefore anything but passive. Silent prayer is not a dream, not even a pious dream. On the contrary, it is a way of tirelessly gathering all one's energy, all one's will, one's desire and one's love and using them to attend to God. If the imagination is left to its wandering without being given too much attention, the will is at the heart of contemplative prayer. Every moment – every little unit of time devoted to saying the name of God internally – is a moment in which the will engages, a moment in which the praying person seeks to be as present as possible, with all our attention, with all our faith. And this is not done without dryness. Francis de Sales spoke of it delicately to a young lady who was trying silent prayer: 'We do not hurry to speak with him because the last time with him was useful to us, but all the more so because it was perhaps less enjoyable for us.'[8]

NOTES

1. *Letter of the Pseudo-Chrysostom to monks* PG 60, p. 752–755. Cited in Lev Gillet, *The Prayer of Jesus: Its Genesis, Development and Practice in the Byzantine-Slavic Religious Tradition,* New York: Desclée, 1967, p. 42.

2. Meister Eckhart, *Sermons & Treatises*, Volume I, translated and edited by M. O'C. Walshe, Longmead: Element Books, 1979. Sermon 6, p. 55.

3. Ibid. Sermon 13b, p. 118.

4. William de Saint-Thierry, *Oraisons méditatives* VII, 1, Paris, Le Cerf, 'Sources chrétiennes', 1985, p. 53. English version by the translator.

5. Theoleptos of Philadelphia, †1320 'On Inner Work in Christ and the Monastic Profession': G.E.H. Palmer, Philip Sherrard, Kallistos Ware (eds), *The Philokalia: The Complete Text*, Volume IV, London: Faber and Faber, 1995, p. 181.

6. John Chapman, *Spiritual Letters*, London: Continuum, 2003, Letter LXXV (Letter 41), p. 180.

7. John Chapman, *Spiritual Letters*, London: Continuum, 2003, Letter LXXV (Letter 41), p. 179.

8. St Francis de Sales, Letter 641 to a young woman [Mlle de Soulfour?] between 1605 et 1608. English version by the translator.

Is it an Effective Form of Prayer?

Effective! Such an adjective may seem utterly inappropriate when it comes to prayer. It is not a question of suggesting that the way proposed here is effective as a technique or in the way a drug can be effective. Again, in the Christian faith, union with God is regarded as a pure gift of God: one can seek to make oneself available but it is not in one's power to make it happen. Also, it is an illusion to look for instruments that can be used to measure the effectiveness of prayer, as though we wanted to evaluate the gift of God. On the other hand, one can try to evaluate the ways that help Christians to enter prayer and to stay with it faithfully. One can try to see how this or that spiritual practice supports them in their spiritual journey, answers their questions, guides them in their quest for God. In that case, we are not evaluating what comes from God but our own contribution.

A WAY OF PRAYER OPEN TO EVERYONE

This way of praying is so simple that it is truly accessible to all. This does not mean that everyone has the desire to practise it. The Christian tradition has developed a rich variety of ways of praying, with the advantage that everyone can find the path that suits them. But for those who wish to have as part of their prayer that extra sense of grace and contemplation, it is a form of prayer that has proved its value over time. One can be a little confused at first by its simplicity, but also, it must be admitted, by its austerity. One may also ask the question: 'Of what use is all this?' We stay silent, we try to be there, and nothing happens ... No inner voices, no illumination, no practical resolutions: apparently, nothing happens. And yet, those who have persevered and who have been practising it for years are unanimous in saying that their lives have changed. Not only has their relationship with God become more reflective and simple, but also their way of life has undergone a transformation.

Two common examples: often people are more comfortable practising this form of meditation in the morning, before embarking on the activities of the day. Some come gradually to decide to get up a little earlier to have time to pray before going to work.

Before getting up earlier, they come to reorganise their sleep, to go to bed a little earlier, watch a little less television, and so, step by step, for the sake of consistency with this privileged time in the presence of God, a new lifestyle evolves and becomes simplified.

Similarly, when this prayer is practised by people with really busy lives, they find that their relationship to their work and their responsibilities also evolves. When one starts their day by doing nothing, and if one considers this sabbatical time essential, one feels a little less the need to run around the rest of the time, to prove oneself at all costs, because we understand that what we are is more important than what we do. 'People', said Meister Eckhart, 'should not worry so much about what they have to do, they should consider rather what they *are*.'[1]

THE DOOR TO SILENCE

It must be said again and again that such a practice is not a path to God but an aid to enter into silence and to be present to God, before, during and after the prayer. Just as prayer does not arouse the presence of God but allows us to be attentive, we could say that it does not produce silence but makes us able to welcome it. The profound silence of this prayer, whether it is practised alone or in a group, should not be regarded as a performance, as a state that one has succeeded in creating, thanks to an irreproachable technique. Silence changes profoundly when it is received as a gift. Various practices may help us to be available and receptive, and such supports should not be underestimated. But silence is a gift, a gift already present before prayer. Our actions do not create it; rather they enable us to engage with the gift and to welcome it.

This access to silence is an area where we can very quickly see a positive development. We can still have trouble keeping quiet, not knowing yet what to do with all the thoughts that cross our mind, but we know at least the path leads to silence. This is the great plus of always praying the same word, the same name. As soon as we begin to say it inwardly, we find the path to interiority, to that silent hinterland of the soul where God awaits us. If a regular time is devoted daily to this practice, then it will be easy to get back into prayer at other times of the day, even briefly – waiting at the bus stop or taking the elevator: these little pauses will allow the name to come back to mind, permitting us to return, for a few moments, to that silent presence of God who is always with us. After many years of practising this form of prayer, one academic said, 'I cannot create silence, but I can receive it and maybe even find it. To receive it, to find it, signifies that it was already there, and that it is not my work.'

Sometimes we are so interested in this access to silence, in the impression of visiting regions little known to ourselves, that we may be tempted to look at what is happening and to pray while observing ourselves. This may be the snare of those who are too focused on the technical aspect of this practice. They have so much desire to do well that they are more attentive to the way of doing things than to the objective pursued. Instead of standing in the presence of God in faith, they never stop watching their posture, their breathing, or observe the variations of both. Some people ask themselves a lot of questions and talk passionately about whether to continue to say the name inwardly if one has reached a state of deep silence. But this is a false question. It is true that this practice, like other forms of prayer, can give rise to moments of profound silence in which there are no more words or images. Saint Thomas Aquinas said:

> Hence then alone should we use words and such like
> signs when they help to excite the mind internally.
> But if they distract or in any way impede the mind
> we should abstain from them.[2]

It should not be that the desire to do well arouses such attention to repeating the name inwardly that it becomes an obstacle to the inner life and silence.

These moments when one experiences a deep silence are rare and probably brief. If we are observing that we are in this silence, it is certain that we are no longer in the silence: we are looking at ourselves, instead of 'looking' at God. It is then preferable to resume the practice of the repetition of the name, to get away from this intense contemplation of oneself.

The great St Francis de Sales was a spiritual master and a realist. He had spotted this flaw that can alter the prayer of one who pays attention to the self at prayer to the point of reducing the prayer to nothing:

> If we pray to God while observing ourselves in
> prayer, we are not being wholly attentive to prayer.
> We are diverting our attention from God, to whom
> we are praying, and thinking instead of the prayer
> by which we are praying. Our preoccupation

with having no distraction often serves as a great distraction to us. Simplicity in spiritual activity is most desirable. Do you want to look at God? Look at him and be attentive to him. But if you reflect and turn your eyes on yourself, to see how you look while looking at him, it is no longer God whom you look at, it is your posture or yourself. He who is in prayer does not know whether he is in prayer or not, for he does not think of the prayer he makes, but of God to whom he makes it. The one who is in the embrace of sacred love does not turn back to look at his heart, to look at himself, to look at what he does, but keeps him focused and engaged with God to whom he directs his love.[3]

In this form of prayer, it is therefore not helpful to 'turn one's eyes on oneself', to look at oneself in order to check that one is doing well. The fruitfulness of this form of prayer develops through faithfulness in the long haul. In general, it is not half an hour of silent prayer that changes a life, but faithfulness to that time for weeks, months, years, no matter what happens.

Most of those who seek to pray are embarrassed by the issue of distractions. They find the thoughts and images that go through their minds during the prayer quite incongruous and dream of finding a way of thinking about nothing. This is a terrible illusion because these phenomena are the signs of cerebral activity and it is not really helpful to dream of a time when the brain would no longer function. Moreover, it is a fundamental mistake about Christian prayer. In this prayer, the believer does not seek extraordinary states of consciousness, he wants to turn to God to welcome and love him, with all that he is, as a pray-er, with his whole human self. He tries to do his best to make himself available, without measuring whether something is changing in him. When a friend is received or visited, this meeting does not lose its value because at times a thought passes through our minds: the essential thing is to be present and do what you can to be attentive to the other, within our limits. To pursue such dreams of emptiness or absolute silence is hopeless and a false path. This can persuade people who think like that that prayer is not for them but is reserved for others. What one must learn to do is not to stop the functioning of one's brain; it is rather to choose tirelessly in faith to give the first place to God. An image runs through my mind, but I turn my inner gaze back to God by turning it away from that image.

How to Sit with God

An idea, a worry takes hold of me, but, Lord, it is in your presence that I want to be at this moment. Dom Chapman wrote:

> The result is naturally that, while our will is making its intense (but almost imperceptible) act of love, our imagination is running about by itself, just as it does in a dream; so that we *seem* to be full of distractions, and not praying at all. But this is the contrary of the fact. The distractions, which are so vivid to us, are not voluntary actions, and have no importance; whereas the *voluntary* action we are performing is the *wanting* God, or giving ourselves to God.[4]

When you drive, you do not become blind to everything that happens on the side of the road; you also see the landscape, the people and the billboards passing by. But, as you drive, you constantly keep your eye in the distance on the road, because that's the most important thing at that moment. What catches your eye in the distance may be beautiful or ugly in some way but this is not the time to look at it. In saying the name of God inwardly, we do the same thing: even though all sorts of ideas can pop up, our attention is not focused on them but on the presence of God to which we return by means of the prayer word. And this is repeated regardless of the thoughts or images that come up, whether beautiful or zany, pious or erotic. We do not stop there, because this is not the time. So there is no analysis to be done, one could almost say no time to lose, wondering why such an idea is there or how the mind has come to such a point. We look at it and we continue on our way. So it is never a question of fighting against thoughts, but of recapturing oneself, thanks to the name, to bring our attention back to the presence of God. In giving a teaching to hermits, Denis the Carthusian already pointed out, in 1451, this need of resumption, of tirelessly recollecting oneself again:

> It is necessary that our souls accustom themselves to recovering quickly, to recollecting themselves in God, to be established more each day in the realities from on high. For that very reason, we attach our heart to some object never to let go again.

> Whenever we realise that we are distracted, tempted, somehow wounded in our thoughts, we must with perseverance take our souls in hand so as not to let them wander aimlessly.[5]

It would not be right to think simply that 'with the word we'll avoid distractions'. This would be to give too much importance, too much profile, to distractions. The effort should not be focused on distractions, to drive them away, but on God, to acknowledge his presence and to love him. If there is, indeed, any effectiveness in this practice, it is not because it stops the thoughts, but because it makes it possible not to remain there, or at least to know how to escape distraction when, suddenly, one becomes aware of the issue.

However, the inner movement that energises the one who prays must not be on the level of a psychological effort, but rather on the level of an impetus towards God. It should be noted that the learning that is done here in prayer is valid for Christian life, both spiritual and moral. It may seem simple, but it is life-changing to finally accept that the Christian tradition teaches that the spiritual struggle is about doing good and not fighting evil.

It can happen that such silent 'doing nothing' triggers the return to the surface of memories and emotions that were thought to have been long forgotten. At the same time, in times of difficulty or conflict, worries force themselves, accompanied by feelings of anger or anguish, and one wonders how one will be able to retain one's prayer time with so much going on. Here again, this is not the time to dwell on these ideas, either to analyse them or to look for solutions. A certain freedom comes from acknowledging such things: it is beneficial to look them in the face, but without delaying for a long time. When you visit a museum, your eyes may fall on the wastebasket or on the fire alarm but you do not stop there, because you have better things to be doing. The bin and the fire alarm, however, are good in themselves, and their presence is justified in this place, but for you, at that moment, these are not what occupy you and so you do not waste your time on them. Your five-year-old boy, who is not a fan of museums, will undoubtedly be very interested in the flashing box or what is in the basket and you will have to develop skills to bring him back to what seems to you more important just now.

Should we spend our prayer time lamenting such thoughts and asking God to free us from them? It is likely that he can do it, if it is really necessary. But we too have our part to play freeing ourselves. Just turn to God, and acknowledge such thoughts – no more – 'It is there, but it is not me, and it's not the heart of the matter.' If we are overwhelmed by memories that arouse guilt or pain, if we come back unreservedly to wounds received or given, it is helpful to turn to God, considering that this movement towards him is infinitely more important that what concerns us. Such things are real and there's no point in denying their reality but they are not the whole story. They cannot define me and they do not constitute the truth of who I am before God.

ATTENTION AND INTENTION

To understand the role of the word, of the name used in prayer, it might help to look at two very similar ideas – attention and intention. Initially, the word is useful to fix our attention on God. Confronted with the uninterrupted flow of thoughts, memories, images, emotions that invade our minds, we find in the repetition of the name a simple means of refocusing ourselves, leaving aside all these thoughts, to replace them, in a way, by that of God. But we cannot limit ourselves to this psychological level. We know very well that such a form of concentration, of mindfulness, can be obtained by the repetition of a word, a mantra, by focusing on a mental image.

Many traditions and methods use this technique to achieve deeper states of consciousness, or to maintain concentration. It can be interesting and useful, but it is not Christian prayer. And it is not enough to fix one's attention on God so that one can really speak of Christian prayer. Even a non-believer, or a believer of another religion, can as well fix his mental attention on God as Christians understand it, or on Christ, without being in a relationship with God or Christ.

If one's goal is prayer and not simply psychological practices, one must move on to another mode of mental functioning, joining intention to attention. The intention here stands for the movement of our whole being towards God. When we pray, we are not content simply to fix our attention psychologically; rather, we do it with love, with the desire to be united to God whose mysterious presence we contemplate. In a passage on Christian meditation, Cardinal Ratzinger described prayer as this encounter between the creature and our God:

> Christian prayer is always determined by the structure of the Christian faith, in which the very truth of God and the creature shines forth. That is

why it presents itself, strictly speaking, as a personal, intimate and profound dialogue between us and God. It thus expresses the communion of redeemed creatures with the intimate life of the Holy Trinity. This communion, which is grounded in Baptism and the Eucharist, the source and summit of the life of the Church, includes an attitude of conversion, an exodus from the 'me' to the 'you' of God.[6]

A WAY OF SAYING THE NAME OF GOD

This has practical consequences for the time spent in silent prayer. On the one hand, it entails a way of saying the name. It is not necessary to say it as many times as possible. It is not the pronunciation of the name that is effective, but the attention of the heart turning confidently to God. It is better then to say it quietly, as one murmurs the name of someone one loves or as one sings the name of a child whom one helps to fall asleep. On the other hand, it is not necessary to associate words with the name of the person being prayed to, because it is really towards him, the living God, that one turns. His name is beyond all names (Phil 2:9).

The name designates who he is, while respecting the incomprehensibility of God's mystery. When the name is pronounced internally, with attention as well as intention, it is naturally laden with all that dwells in us. Some days it will be pronounced as a cry for help, at other times as a cry of joy, anguish or anger. Sometimes also it will be said in great peace, as one rests in trust in the hands of him from whom we have nothing to fear.

Our intention takes a whole variety of forms, while praying the very same word. In that way, silent prayer is always new and never boring. We say the same word and, at the same time, we don't feel that it is just the same each time.

In the seventeenth century, this was called the 'prayer of simple regard'[7] – a way of staying in the presence of God, without elaborate thoughts. Some spiritual writers encouraged the repetition of a word to support this simple gaze on God. In his treatise on contemplation, a Benedictine monk emphasised the connection between the simplicity of the practice and the orientation of the heart towards God:

> When we speak of the prayer of simple regard, we must not imagine that this 'look' is absolutely necessary. It is simple, because it does not involve thoughts, concepts and a plethora of ideas, but, at the

same time, it is not simple, because it is accompanied by a very pure and very perfect love of God. This focus on God, this seeing or looking at God, this application of the self to God ever present is really the 'matter'[8] of this prayer, while the 'form' is love, the movement of the heart and the inner desire for God.[9]

MEASURING THE EFFECTIVENESS OF THIS PRAYER

After we recognise how much this form of silent prayer can lead us towards inner silence and how much it can help us in the struggle with distractions, is there some way we can evaluate our prayer? It is true that a way of praying must not only help us to pray, during the time of prayer itself, it must also lead to changes in the life of the Christian. What is the use of deepening one's capacity for silence if one does not grow in faith and love? From a Christian perspective, a particular spirituality can only be considered effective if it shows its fruitfulness in everyday life and in our relationships with others. Love is a much more important matter than access to this or that state of consciousness.

The first criterion is always that of love. In the spiritual life, as in all aspects of the Christian life, it is the essential criterion for right behaviour and conduct, increasing our capacity to love God, our neighbour and ourselves. Likewise, in silent prayer, where we do not give much importance to what is felt in the time of prayer, we can say that we prayed well, not because we felt a great warmth or inner perception of a great light, but because, coming out of prayer, we are stronger in our service of our brother and sister. 'In fact, genuine prayer, as the great spiritual masters teach, stirs up in the person who prays an ardent charity which moves him to collaborate in the mission of the Church and to serve his brothers for the greater glory of God.'[10] Here again the means and the methods are not without interest, but they must always be viewed as secondary realities in relation to the essential.

Many Christian spiritual writers, such as Eckhart, Francis de Sales, Vincent de Paul and many others have pointed out that, when we are at prayer and charity calls us to serve someone poor or sick, we should 'leave God for God'. As we 'abandon' loving God in prayer, we continue to love God in fraternal charity:

As I have said before, if a man were in an ecstasy as St Paul was (2 Cor 12:2-4), and if he knew of a sick person who needed a bowl of soup from him, I would consider it far better if you were to leave that rapture out of love and help the needy person out of greater love. A man should not suppose that in this way he is bereft of grace for, whatever a man willingly gives up for love, he shall be received in nobler fashion; as Christ says: 'He who leaves anything for my sake will receive again a hundredfold' (Mt 19:29).[11]

Christianity refuses to separate the spiritual quest from human relationships. To look at prayer or this or that form of meditation – considering it only as a method of personal development – is a serious misconception. We then make a relationship with God an instrument in the service of our own well-being – in reality, a form of idolatry. This tendency leads in any case to a dead-end because we find our ultimate fulfilment only in relationship with others.

Let us return to the seventeenth century, where prayer was an inexhaustible subject of discussion, and where many Christians were attracted to a form of very austere prayer called 'prayer of simple regard'. It was a prayer very close to the prayer we are talking about here. While remaining quiet and silent, the believer was approaching God with a simple look of faith, without trying to meditate or understand this or that aspect of the mystery. She stood there quietly in the presence of God. Father Guilloré has, on this subject, given us criteria of discernment which are very useful for us today.[12] He insists on the necessary integration of lived behaviour and simple prayer, by sharply questioning the quality of the prayer of simple regard of those people whose behaviour in daily life is totally lacking in humility, simplicity and restraint. In his opinion, gossip, superficiality and exaggerated sensitivity are unmistakable signs that we are fooling ourselves.

The account he gives of people deluding themselves is not without resonance today. In particular, he emphasises that those who believe that they live this form of prayer, yet, like to talk endlessly about the spiritual life, to communicate their inner life in detail, to tell of their experiences to anyone who will listen, are, in fact, merely showing their lack of competence! Silent prayer is a source of silence and discretion, it fosters a certain reserve, a lack of pretension that can be seen in every aspect of life.

Father Guilloré also emphasises how much this form of simple prayer casts a bright light on our faults and on our complexes. Every authentic spiritual step is also accompanied by an experience of truth about oneself. It does not immerse the believer in low self-esteem but by placing the self more explicitly before the holiness of God, it reveals to each their own limits and failings. Such disappointment that one may feel at not being able to remain in the presence of God for some time, without paying attention to the minor worries or conflicts that occupy our minds, is at the same time the source of true humility. It saves us from thinking we are great mystics and reminds us that union *with* God is a gift *from* God.

Without him, we could do nothing.

If my practice of prayer makes me aggressive towards those who disturb me, and unavailable to serve those who are waiting for my help, it is essential to break free from such an approach.

Love – the ability to put oneself at the service of one's neighbour – is the essential criterion that makes it possible to measure the quality of one's prayer.

Everything else is secondary.

DON'T WASTE TIME WITH CONTRADICTIONS!

Once the primacy of love is affirmed, let us seek to be in the presence of God with good will and let's not observe ourselves at prayer to see if it is any good. With his inimitable gentleness and firmness, the great St Francis de Sales was unparalleled in bringing directees to the heart of the matter, setting people free from their desire to excel. This is the advice he gives to Jeanne de Chantal about her prayer:

> Be always faithful in this resolution to remain in very simple union and unique simplicity in the presence of God, by giving yourself completely to his most holy will, and whenever you find your mind has wandered, bring yourself back gently, without doing any conscious acts of understanding or will. This simple, trusting love, this surrender and repose of your spirit in the fatherly embrace of Our Lord and his providence, includes in a wonderful way all that we may desire in uniting ourselves with God. Stay like that without thinking about what you are doing or will do, or what will happen to you, and indeed about any other eventuality.

How to Sit with God

Do not worry too much about your contradictions and afflictions, but take everything from the hand of God, without exception, remaining gentle, patient, and simply surrendering to his holy will. May all your words and actions be accompanied by gentleness and simplicity. When you notice some care or concern, give it back to God, seeking only him and the doing of his holy will, leaving him to take care of all the rest. Remain in solitude and simplicity before our Lord Jesus Christ crucified.[13]

NOTES

1. Meister Eckhart, *Sermons & Treatises,* Volume III, translated and edited by M. O'C. Walshe, Longmead: Element Books, 1979; Talks of Instruction 4, p. 14.

2. Thomas Aquinas, *Summa Theologica*, IIa IIæ, q. 83, a. 12.

3. St Francis de Sales, *Traité de l'amour de Dieu*, IX, X. English version by the translator.

4. John Chapman, *Spiritual Letters*, London: Continuum, 2003, Letter LXXV (Letter 41), p. 180.

5. Denis the Carthusian, *Livre de vie des recluses* [1451], III, trad. Louis-Albert Lassus, Paris, Beauchesne, 2003. English version by the translator.

6. Joseph Ratzinger, *Letter to the Bishops of the Catholic Church on Some Aspects of Christian Meditation*, 15 October 1989, §3.

7. See pages 160-161.

8. The distinction between matter and form designates what is determined and what determines. Here, the inclination of the heart towards God determines a behaviour, the simple look or regard.

9. André Rayez, 'Le traité de la contemplation de Dom Claude Martin', Revue ascétique et mystique, 115, 1953, p. 206–249. Citation p. 224. English version by the translator.

10. Joseph Ratzinger, *Letter to the Bishops of the Catholic Church on some Aspects of Christian Meditation*, 15 October 1989, §28.

11. Meister Eckhart, *Sermons & Treatises,* Volume III, translated and edited by M. O'C. Walshe, Longmead: Element Books, 1979; Sermon 13b, p. 118; Talks of Instruction 10, p. 72.

12. François Guilloré, *Conférences spirituelles pour bien mourir à soi-même*, tome premier, à Paris, chez Étienne Michallet, premier imprimeur du Roy, rue S. Jacques à l'image S. Paul près la fontaine S. Séverin, MDCLXXXIX, p. 337 V, p. 317–343.

13. Advice of St Francis de Sales to Mother Jeanne de Chantal, 6 June 1616, opuscule XXV. English version by the translator.

How to Do It?

This form of prayer is both rigorous in its practice and, at the same time, very flexible. If we want to go deeper, we must find a way to keep ourselves in silence for at least twenty minutes, without having to move, as we turn our whole being towards God, thanks to the inner repetition of the familiar name of God. It is good to hold firmly to this discipline. After that the practical question of where one prays, the time which is most suitable, whether to do it with others or alone – all these factors vary a great deal.

PRAYING ALONE

Silent prayer can be done in groups but the usual daily practice is alone, with the exception of some special communities. Those who recognise in this way a prayer path that suits them will have to find the practical settings that will allow them to pray every day. Although this form of prayer can be done under a wide variety of conditions – such as while travelling or on holiday – precisely because it does not require any particular equipment, it is nevertheless facilitated by a regular format each day: a place, a time, a position, a small personal ritual for the beginning and the end of this moment devoted to God.

A PLACE FOR PRAYER

When we want to put in place a regular practice of prayer, it is a great help to do our prayer in the same place. It doesn't matter where – in your room, a quiet corner of the house, the local church if open – the key really is to find a spot that promotes tranquillity and prayer. It is not that God is more present here than elsewhere; simply, this is a place that helps us.

Meister Eckhart said:

> A man may go out into the fields and say his prayers and know God, or he may go to church and know God; but if he is more aware of God because he is in a quiet place, as is usual, that comes from his imperfection and not from God; for God is equally in all things and all places.[1]

Similarly, everyone can find ways of embellishing this place of prayer – a candle, an image, flowers, simple things, which do not require time or effort to install. The sanctuary where God wants to be worshipped, says Jesus to the Samaritan woman, is the human heart. So the material conditions are there to favour the contemplation. They can be adjusted according to the taste of the individual and should never become indispensable. In a word, we should be able to adore God, in spirit and in truth, anywhere.

Without being identical, our days do resemble each other, as do our weeks. It helps a lot to bring prayer into the rhythms of everyday life. Some are morning people, while others feel the evening more suitable. One size definitely does not fit all! On the other hand, it is difficult to be faithful to daily prayer without establishing a certain rhythm.

If you decide to pray when you feel like it, or when you have time, you will not pray often. Moreover, such an attitude places your own desire at the source of prayer. Such a foundation would be very fragile for a human relationship. Do we take care of our children only when we want to or merely when we find the time? Do we make ourselves available to those we love only when it suits ourselves? We take our responsibilities seriously because we have to, because it is normal, and because we know that we would deny ourselves if we were lacking in this regard.

It is good to consider prayer also in this way: an appointment with God, which creates a sense of priority. There are always many other things to do at prayer time. Important and urgent things, things we would even prefer to do. But if we make the choice, day after day, to stick to what we have decided – that is, to do nothing, with God and for God, for a moment – it becomes evident that this time dedicated to God is what is most important. Father Le Saux, a Benedictine monk in India, wrote:

> Moments consecrated by man to this special and silent prayer are indeed an offering to God ... These times are the highest form of 'sacrifice' ... the highest act of worship.[2]

Faithfulness depends also on the amount of time each day we devote to prayer. If the duration of the prayer depends on how I feel, it is likely to be shorter and shorter, because I feel nothing. And if one day I am upset or sleepy, I will tend to extend the time. Here again, in doing so, one places oneself in the centre, instead of giving that place to God. It may seem formal to fix a specific length of time and to stick to it, whatever happens, whether boredom or ecstasy. But it is the best way to sustain fidelity, and to honour that moment when everything stops because it is a time given to God. Thus we respond to the call of Psalm 45: 'Be still and know that I am God.'

The recommended duration for prayer is twenty-five minutes. It takes at least twenty minutes for any kind of substantial prayer. If prayer time is meant to be a pause in the presence of God, we must take the time to really experience the moment that elapses, thus breaking with the rhythm of the rest of the day. If the break lasts five minutes, it will not really feel like a break. On the other hand, it is recommended not to hold the same motionless posture for more than thirty minutes because one is likely to become stiff and it may even lead to problems of circulation. A twenty-five minute prayer time is therefore a happy medium.

If, at the start, the prayer time seems a bit long, it is possible to start with a period of shorter duration, say about ten minutes. Over this brief period, set up the posture, the way of praying, the daily practice of faithfulness. It is very likely that quite soon you will feel the need to increase the duration a little, up to twenty-five minutes. Such is the experience of many who have gone before you. But in any case, what is most important to the spirit of this prayer is to do it for a certain time, which is not subject to change every day.

During a retreat, or on holidays, it is possible to pray for a longer period and if one feels the desire to remain in silent prayer for a longer stretch, one can stitch together twenty-five minute units while taking a few minutes of physical relaxation between each unit. A very slow walk around the room, for example, allows you to take a little exercise without leaving the realm of interiority which is that of prayer. Some people appreciate this very special walking practice that comes from Zen: it consists of taking one foot off the ground (only once the other is firmly on the ground!) and doing so as slowly as possible.

HOW TO START AND HOW TO END

A small personal ritual is observed by all who practise this prayer, to mark the beginning and end of the prayer. Some people need to have a time in between, to get out of their activities, by putting on some music, for example, or doing some yoga exercises. Others read a text from the Bible or from a spiritual author, either before the prayer or as a conclusion. The Lord's Prayer can introduce it, as recommended by St Teresa of Ávila. It can also be the conclusion. It is up to everyone to see what suits him or her according to temperament, place and time of prayer.

Then there is the question of how to measure prayer time. It can indeed be very uncomfortable for the person praying to have one's watch placed in front of oneself and to observe the hand moving, while lamenting that it does not go faster. It is essential, especially for beginners, to be free from concern about time. If one lives next to a town hall or a church that rings the hours, it may be possible to use this sound to end the session if the prayer is made at the same time every day. If you choose an instrument to measure the time – alarm clock, timer, mobile phone – you have to make sure that the audible signal is not too abrupt, because it is likely to startle you when it rings. Today, it is also possible to record a sequence including a start signal (gong, bell, Bible verse …), twenty-five minutes of silence, and an end signal.[3] This eliminates the need to make daily adjustments to your alarm clock; just switch on a computer or iPod to play the sequence. In short, all improvements are to be encouraged, as long as they free us from worrying about the timing.

AND IF ONE LETS THE PRACTICE DROP?

The practice of silent prayer may appear at times somewhat austere, but what form of prayer does not? We set up a place, a time, and start with good intentions of faithfulness, and then the excitement dulls. One morning we stay in bed, then we go on vacation, and we eventually realise that it has been three months since we last prayed. Must we conclude that such prayer is impossible, that it is too difficult and that it was wrong to think of oneself as a mystic? It would be a pity, because all those who undertake the adventure of prayer experience such doubts. Just because we have been praying regularly for years does not mean that we are somehow safe from such slippage. Holidays, in particular, are terrible times for prayer. We always believe that we will have more time, that it will be easier but it turns out to be quite the opposite. The change of rhythm, the change of pace, the disorganisation of the days are really averse to the regular pattern.

As soon as one realises that the prayer session has been abandoned for two days, two weeks or two months, the only thing to do is to sit down and start again. In the time of prayer itself, our attention to God is sustained as best we can, in spite of all the images and distractions enticing us elsewhere. Something similar can happen over longer periods of days and years when our faithfulness falls into failure and forgetfulness. Again, we don't dwell on this and we draw no conclusions, with the exception of the call to start again. With great patience, a certain habit is put in place, but it is not a protection against forgetting or failure. It just makes you more aware that something is lacking in a day when the usual prayer time has been missed. The day lacks a centre of gravity, you catch yourself overworking and getting excited over little things. Has silent prayer had no place for a few days, a few weeks, a few months?

Awareness of this should not lead to a feeling of unworthiness or discouragement. All that is required is to take oneself in hand and find again the path of prayer, even starting like a beginner again, as we discover once more our taste for silence.

GROUP PRAYER

Many practitioners of silent prayer enjoy being able to pray with others, either during a single session or at regular meetings. This group practice is not a substitute for solitary prayer: going to a group in this way without practising at home can be very disenchanting. We expect the community to do what we do not do for ourselves. This sets up an unhealthy dependence on the community. On the other hand, if you try to pray every day, it can be very sustaining to find other people with whom to share this experience from time to time.

HOW TO SET UP GROUP MEDITATION

How to set up a group for silent prayer matters a great deal. Even more than in personal prayer, it is necessary to be clear about what one is doing. It is possible to welcome believers of another religion into a time of Christian silent prayer if they agree to participate. To share the silence (under the pretext of welcoming all), without making it clear *what* we are doing and *in whose name* we are doing it, is much more hazardous precisely because of the lack of clarity.

For a time of quiet Christian prayer, a relatively neutral place will be better than a chapel, so that Christians of different faiths can feel at ease and that everyone can take the posture that suits him or her without being bothered by the sacred character of the place. A representation of Christ will be highlighted, as the centre towards which all turn, avoiding the violent representations evoking the crucifixion in an explicit way. An icon or a photo of a Romanesque Christ, for example, might be appropriate. If you have a large Bible, you can also gather the group around it, the book being open on a stand or low table before you.

The participants place themselves as they please, turned towards the centrepiece set up before their arrival. The group could form a sort of horseshoe shape, around the representation of Christ. Those who need to sit on a chair take their place in the outer ring, while those who pray on the ground may sit in the centre.

Small benches or cushions should be provided. It is important that chairs are always available so that anyone who comes for the first time does not feel that sitting on the floor is obligatory. A fairly spacious room is preferable, because the time of prayer can be somewhat oppressive if one is too close to others in a relatively small room. If there are several prayer sessions in a row, doors and windows are opened during the breaks to air the room and to allow people to arrive or leave unobtrusively.

WHO LOOKS AFTER THE TIMING?

In a group prayer, it is essential to have someone who takes responsibility for the prayer, indicating the beginning and the end, and keeping an eye on the time. This serves to free up the other participants. In a group that meets regularly, it is not essential that it is always the same person who provides this service. It is best to avoid ringing devices that sometimes have to be used to measure time when you are alone. To give the signal for the beginning and the end of the silence, the most suitable sound is that of the gong, or the 'singing bowls' that are easily found in Asian stores. This gives a sober sound, which will not startle the participants, as long as you do not strike it too hard. The long reverberation of the bronze gong makes one aware of the silence which settles gradually on the group.

For group prayer, it is vital to insist on the rule that no one enters the room once the prayer has begun. It is good to make this really clear by leaving the room door open as long as possible to let people in and then closing it when the time for prayer has started. Nobody is obliged to participate, but if we want to pray with others, we should be present from the start. In the deep silence of group prayer, the arrival of a latecomer takes us out of the inner silence. When the prayer is over, we open the door once more. This is especially important if you have several prayer sessions in a row.

At each break, we open the door to allow those who wish to join the group to do so and those who wish to leave the room to do likewise. For that same reason, it is also important to make it clear that we do not leave the room during prayer, except in an emergency. These ground rules should be clearly stated, and possibly displayed on the door, so that the silence of the group is not disturbed by participants who think they are being inconspicuous.

HOW TO BEGIN AND HOW TO END?

As in personal prayer, there is great room here for creativity. Some groups do some yoga exercises; others listen to a text. Another successful practice, once everyone is settled, is to read a very brief text, like a scripture verse or a quotation from a spiritual text, and then to sound the gong. Twenty-five minutes later, a second gong lets people move, but without getting up again, until another short reading is offered, sometimes the same one used at the start. A final stroke of the gong signals the end of the prayer time, allowing everyone to get up at their own pace.

This punctuation of *time* by a word has its importance. It resembles that of the marking of the sacred space by a Christian symbol. Before entering the silence, the group hears a word, because in the Christian perspective, human prayer, even silent, is always a response to a word that comes before it. The word reveals to us creatures the proximity of God and lets us know that we are precious in God's eyes. Silent prayer, simply punctuated by this minimal but crucial word that is the name of God, is a response to the word we have heard. At the same time, it prepares us to hear the word that will be proclaimed again at the end. These short texts, received in silence, really do stay in our minds and hearts.

NOTES

1. Meister Eckhart, *Sermons & Treatises*, Volume II, translated and edited by M. O'C. Walshe, Longmead: Element Books, 1979; Sermon 69, p. 69.

2. Abhishiktananda/Henri Le Saux, OSB, *Prayer*, Philadelphia: The Westminster Press, 1969, p. 31.

3. You can download such sequences at www.priere-silencieuse.org. Many sites in English offer a similar service (translator).

It is a Struggle and a Discipline

One of the prayers used during Mass asks God to 'give us grace to serve you always with joy, because our full and lasting happiness is to make of our lives a constant service to the author of all that good'.[1] Our joy and happiness are to serve the Lord in faithfulness: here is a beautiful programme for the spiritual life. Quite often, those who wish to give prayer a more important place in their lives do not do so because they imagine they have to perform spiritual feats, demanding several hours a day, experiencing ecstasy once a week. Once they realise that the reality of their lives does not correspond to this dream, they conclude that prayer is not for them.

The foundation of our faithfulness in prayer is humility. We can serve God faithfully if we have chosen a way of serving him that is realistic, compatible with who we are and with our way of life. It is more fruitful to pray for ten minutes a day for ten years than to dream that one could do three hours a day and despair of ever getting there. There is something a little humbling about committing to give God ten minutes a day and noticing that we do not always succeed. The spiritual struggle will then be to start all over again, tirelessly, without lamenting the days or weeks when the rhythm was lost.

To sustain our daily faithfulness, in all its simplicity, we need some reference points, some rules of life: the same place at a fixed time and the familiar form that prayer takes. Anyone who thinks he will pray when he has time will never pray. Faithfulness calls for a certain discipline, which today can appear contrary to authenticity or spontaneity. Yet we are ready to accept it when it comes to dieting or keeping fit! In the case of physical exercise, as in the spiritual life, one can only progress at the cost of a regular daily effort. It is not the extraordinary experiences that make the life of prayer, but the humble fidelity to it every day, lived over many years. There is no mystery here: those who manage to pray every day are those who give themselves some rules to which they commit themselves. This discipline is not meant to be a straitjacket! It will be applied with flexibility and recognise that travel, illness or simply the unexpected will cause some variation. The paradox is that our loyalty depends as much on our discipline as on our ability to remain flexible and adaptable. If we impose on ourselves an iron discipline, one day or the other, circumstances will knock us off our perch. If we imagine we can always adapt to the immediate circumstances, we will not get very far. It is the balance between discipline and adaptability that sustains us in the long run.

A rule will help to make things a bit more objective. If you commit to give time to God each day so as to remain freely in his presence, does it matter how strongly you feel about praying or not praying? Not at all!

KEEP TO THIS RULE

To give oneself a rule makes it possible to firm things up a little. If you make the commitment to give God time each day so as to remain freely in his presence, keep to this rule, whether you feel holy or not, or whether you feel like praying or not. Bit by bit, this changes everything because your starting point is not you or your state of mind, but God, in whose presence you place yourself. With a liberating simplicity, Denis the Carthusian wrote in the fifteenth century: 'When it's time to pray, let's pray; to work, let's work; to speak, let's speak; to be silent, let's be silent ...'

THE DISCIPLINE OF PRAYER

Putting in place such supports to keep ourselves faithful may seem to be a discipline limited to the spiritual life. Most of those who practise it do so at first to promote their life of prayer. And they are sometimes surprised to see that, gradually, the introduction of a regular prayer time brings about deeper changes in their lifestyle.

Many prefer, for example, to devote to silent prayer a time in the morning, before leaving for work. It is easier than you think to find twenty or twenty-five minutes free at that time. You can simply go to bed half an hour earlier. One can also decide to spend five minutes less in the shower, to get up ten minutes earlier and to spend less time at breakfast, and the time for prayer is made available. At first it's a little awkward and then, quickly enough, we discover that new habits are established and that what seemed impossible becomes part and parcel of our morning ritual. Others realise that a small remodelling of their home would allow them to set aside this time without disturbing their spouse or without being distracted by children waking up. Little by little, small changes take place, supported by the chosen time of prayer. These are not shattering professional reconversions, but small things that make it easier to practise prayer or to lead a life which incorporates prayer.

LEARNING TO BE FREE

Seeking to be attentive in the presence of God: this way of praying may seem very simple, perhaps even too simple. Yet regular practice of such prayer is an amazing route to freedom. We can go far by going nowhere! Even when the time frame, the practical arrangements and the content of this prayer are very stable and regular, this does not lead to stagnation. How is that? By repeating the name of God inwardly, we advance, because we try to avoid everything that could hinder us, everything that would take the place of God.

PERSONAL FREEDOM

One of the most difficult aspects of Christian spiritual struggle is to find a proper relationship with oneself. How to love oneself without falling into selfishness, while respecting in one's self the one who is created in the image of God and loved by God? It can be hard to establish the balance between paying too much attention to the self and paying too little.

To create a healthy attitude, it is essential to know oneself. Freedom comes through knowing ourselves and seeing ourselves as we really are. The silence of prayer and the absence of anything that usually distracts can lead to the emergence of all sorts of surprising things: memories that were thought to have been forgotten, emotions which assume an important place, images that become haunting. In the face of all this Eckhart gives precious advice: 'Observe yourself, and wherever you find yourself, leave yourself. That is the very best way.'[2] Without being afraid of it, we can look in the face of all that lives inside us and that comes back to the surface, while not letting oneself be absorbed by it: it is there in me, but it is not me. This is not the essence of myself, and in any case, this is not the moment, because my focus is on God.

What is true of feelings is also true of the relation to one's own body. This should not become an obsession and should not be the central focus of the person praying. But the best way to get there is to start paying attention. To know how one is built, what one needs to be able to keep quiet. Here, as elsewhere, detachment does not lead to disdain, but on the contrary to freedom as we get to know ourselves. To say that the body does not occupy the essential place does not mean we may pretend it does not exist. Yet many Western Christians look suspiciously at bodily practices associated with prayer: they consider them a waste of time, somehow stolen from God. They commit themselves to prayer and their exclusively spiritual approach is soon hampered by realities which, in their eyes, were not supposed to be part of it: cramps, pains, itching. It would be more realistic, once again, to start from this unavoidable dimension of our being, to get to know the self, to undergo necessary schooling so as to arrive at a bodily freedom which will at last make it possible to be really available.

Once again, it must be underlined that such insights, which are made from the perspective of prayer, have a wider usefulness. If one learns to leave one's emotions, feelings or memory in the right place in the context of prayer, one will gradually become capable of better self-control in everyday life. We spend a few months moving forward in the midst of emotions or hare-brained ideas and one day we discover that we have become more focused on our work and less subject to emotions. It is not that we lose our feelings but we have learned not to be overwhelmed by them.

THE SPIRITUAL STRUGGLE

It is particularly important today to emphasise that prayer is indeed a struggle and remains so throughout life. An additional paradox is that, while the struggle is real, it is at the same time delightful. It is not a question of fighting oneself, or of fighting against oneself, but a question of 'desiring God', as both Eckhart and Catherine of Siena said. The struggle is towards self-knowledge, to know how to take oneself gently, to learn to refocus oneself tirelessly on God, while everything else tends towards a feeling of being scattered.

As soon as one hears about fighting, one thinks of tensions, wilfulness, inability to accept the gift of God and so on. But prayer is a test, like Jacob's wrestling with the angel, because it brings the human being face-to-face with God, bringing together the fallen creature with the holiness of the creator. It is not easy for us to remain a long time in that space. We do everything to escape the ordeal, because God's presence exposes the truth about ourselves. In the text already quoted on Christian meditation, Cardinal Ratzinger spoke of the struggle of prayer:

> For the person who makes a serious effort there will, however, be moments in which he seems to be wandering in a desert and, in spite of all his efforts, he 'feels' nothing of God. He should know that these trials are not spared anyone who takes prayer seriously. However, he should not immediately see this experience, common to all Christians who pray, as the 'dark night' in the mystical sense. In any case in these moments, his prayer, which he will resolutely strive to keep to, could give him the impression of a certain 'artificiality', although really it is something totally different: in fact it is at that very moment an expression of his fidelity to God, in whose presence he wishes to remain even when he receives no subjective consolation in return. In these apparently negative moments, it becomes clear what the person who is praying really seeks: is he indeed looking for God who, in his infinite freedom, always surpasses him; or is he only seeking himself.[3]

Blocks and hindrances in prayer can happen at different levels. Starting with the 'outer', there is bodily fatigue, illness and physical pain. Each of these can trigger quite humbling situations in which we find ourselves unable to pray – for example when suffering from something so ordinary as a toothache. In fact, any of the outward dimensions of prayer can get in the way and become a test, a struggle for faithfulness. A case in point could be the noise level where I pray or even the place where I live. Something similar happens when the outer invades the inner. At times the cares of the world – real or exaggerated – flood our whole being, taking over our longing, our minds and our wills. Then, we really cannot pray and we limp on with the help of a few fundamental formulae. As long as we have not yet experienced faithfulness as sheer doggedness, we do not know much about the spiritual combat.

A subtler difficulty, but just as formidable, is that which arises from the questions about the meaning of prayer. It is the test *par excellence* of those who dedicate their lives to prayer in the monastic life. One day or another, comes the question, 'What's the point?' Is prayer really useful? Is it not a waste of time in relation to the effective service of the poor?

Cannot God save people without prayer, and anyway, when we see how the world is going, can we really say that prayer hastens the coming of the Kingdom? This radical questioning sometimes puts a stop – temporary or lasting – to the practice of prayer, no matter how regular, especially when prayers seem to go unheeded.

The third order of difficulty lies in finding the right place for the intellect. If the mind takes up too much of prayer, prayer is no longer prayer because it dries up and dies in thinking. If the intellect is too little present, the prayer fumbles around in the emotions and feelings because it is not nourished, feeding itself only on the imagination of the person at prayer. This too leads to a death!

One could become too focused, too anxious and too worried about what to do. The one who wishes too much to be a good servant ends by taking care of the self a great deal and paying little attention to God. This is not the way to truly give one's self.

Prayer can easily devolve into a monologue in which one contemplates oneself in the act of praying, one's successes (as the Pharisee in the Gospel), even one's sins and failures (that is, 'scrupulosity'). While we really seek to contemplate God, prayer must eventually arrive at the point of consenting to *not* knowing, *not* seeking but on the contrary *to being found* by the one we seek.

All these struggles and many more mark the spiritual itinerary of those who undertake the adventure of prayer. No technique will spare us such trials except the 'technique' of giving up on our faithfulness, thus avoiding the test of truth. Each of us goes through them in our own way, aware of the path we have to follow. Dialogue with other believers, making the journey in the company of a great spiritual Christian author, all this can help to ask the right questions and to identify the blocks which stand in our way.

After many years of daily fidelity to silent prayer, a man wrote on the occasion of his eightieth birthday:

> At last! I found the Way, I thought ... A few years later,
> I realised that I was on the path that leads to the way.
> The years have passed, I was only on the path leading to the way ...
> Today, with my back bowed, I thank you, Lord, for letting me discover the entrance to the way ...

PEACE OR SERENITY?

Very often today, serenity is presented as the sign of a deep spiritual life. A superficial knowledge of Eastern philosophy suggests that it presents the wise person passing through life totally unaware of the world and its tragedies. An equally superficial rejection of the Christian tradition gives rise to the conviction that Christianity is incapable of leading to serenity and that spiritual life is always marked by penance. In the face of these all too common caricatures, some clarification is called for. The Christian tradition has always recognised peace as a fruit of the Spirit, as a sign that the believer is responding to the call of God. Is this peace identifiable with serenity as it is understood today? What is referred to as serenity is an ability to take a step back from emotions, not to allow oneself to be invaded by the flow of feelings. It may demonstrate some self control or some maturity which is obviously favourable to the spiritual life. This is, however, on the level of psychology and does not promote integration with the Other. But in this area, as in all circumstances, Christianity seeks the criterion of perfection in love.

Mastery of the self doesn't matter if it does not lead to openness to a neighbour in need. Serenity is not a sign of the depth of the spiritual life if it renders one incapable of compassion and practical commitment to the weakest and the most deprived.

Peace is more than an internal state. The Gospel proclaims the peace*makers* happy: peace is a work and not a state. It is an activity rather than a feeling. One of the great masters of Western spirituality, St Francis de Sales, was known for his gentleness and goodness. He had a unique way, in his extensive correspondence, of giving advice, of taking up his interlocutors when he considered that they have gone down a dead end. He always did so with a tone of great gentleness, sometimes even with a little humour, which might lead one to overlook the forthrightness of his position. But it is essential to know that the sweetness of St Francis was the fruit of an immense struggle. Saint Francis de Sales did not have an easy temperament. He was capable of exploding like everyone else and it was only through hard work on himself that he acquired this capacity to be a peacemaker, to say what is true without hurting or offending the one who is struggling on the way.

The path of prayer *can* lead to peace. This will not release you from surface storms or from the troubles of this world. Prayer does not take away feelings because it does not cut you off from your surroundings. But by placing ourselves in the presence of what is essential, by refocusing on the relationship with God no matter what the circumstances, prayer gradually gives rise to an ability to stay the course, even if one is engaged in full-on conflict or in the middle of some human tragedy. In order to understand this, we must imagine that we are a little like an onion, with layer after layer surrounding a core. The centre can be at peace, knowing we are there in the presence of God, our rock, our strength, while the outer layers can be in deep turmoil. While we cannot avoid the storm, we can make sure that its troubles do not invade us too deeply. This is what Eckhart taught the Dominican novices, who were advised to go out from their communities to preach:

> Keep the same attitude that you have in church or in your cell, and carry it with you in the crowd and in unrest and inequality. And – as I have often said – when we speak of 'equality', this does not mean that one should regard all works as equal, or all places or people. That would be quite wrong, for praying is a better task than spinning and the church a nobler

place than the street. But in your acts you should have an equal mind, an equal faith and equal love for your God, and equal seriousness. Assuredly, if you were equal-minded in this way, then no man could keep you from having God ever present.[4]

WE DO NOT PRAY TO BECOME GOOD

We do not pray to become good for that would be to instrumentalise prayer and to make God into a kind of medication. Prayer is not of the order of the useful.

When we ask people who have been praying silently every day for years why they do it, often they do not know what to say. All they know is that their lives would not be the same without that time. This empty space, this Sabbath at the heart of the activity, modifies the meaning of all the rest, without the modification being clearly perceptible or sought. Dom Le Saux wrote:

> Such times of inner recollection are the most truly effective moments of our life. It is towards them that everything else in human life is directed, but they themselves have no ulterior object. It is the greatest mistake to suppose that moments devoted to silent prayer are merely a preparation for our

work. Meditation, for instance, is not intended to make us capable of worthily fulfilling our duties of study, work, or social intercourse, nor even to assist our progress in humility or any other virtue. Contemplation is worthwhile in itself. It needs no further justification. No doubt such high times of prayer will cast their rays on the whole of life, but this radiation will not be deliberately intended. It will happen quite spontaneously …[5]

When monks sing the Psalms of the office seven times a day, it doesn't matter how they feel. One can even say that if they are too attentive to themselves, there is little chance they will be able to sing together properly. The spiritual experience peculiar to the common prayer of the office is that it takes the focus off one's self. 'The work of God,' as the Rule of St Benedict calls it, must be accomplished and the work must be done well.

Thus, throughout the days and years, the community builds its unity and the monk is steeped in the Word he sings. Silent prayer is part of the same attitude: during the time of prayer, I do not seek to analyse what is happening in me. Instead, I try to be there, to be completely present in what I am doing, that is to say, staying in the presence of God, focusing all my attention on him. Some days are difficult and it can be extremely hard to concentrate, to stay in one place, or to not let our thoughts return to the problems that are bothering us. Silent prayer is then a fight at every moment, where, each time the name is repeated, it is necessary to take oneself again in hand and to bring oneself back in the presence of God. We come out exhausted, wondering if it was worth it. The answer is obviously yes: we may not have found serenity, but we sought God with good will. These small acts of faith repeated in turmoil, while so many other concerns (often legitimate) occupy the mind, have a deep value. They can nourish peace of mind, even if our goal is not that but rather God alone.

NOTES

1. Opening Prayer at Mass for the thirty-third week in Ordinary Time.

2. Meister Eckhart, *Sermons & Treatises*, Volume III, translated and edited by M. O'C. Walshe, Longmead: Element Books, 1979; Talks of Instruction 3, p. 14.

3. Joseph Ratzinger, *Letter to the Bishops of the Catholic Church on some Aspects of Christian Meditation*, 15 October 1989, §30.

4. Meister Eckhart, *Sermons & Treatises*, Volume III, translated and edited by M. O'C. Walshe, Longmead: Element Books, 1979; Talks of Instruction no. 6, p. 17.

5. Abhishiktananda/Henri Le Saux, OSB, Prayer, Philadelphia: The Westminster Press, 1969, p. 25.

One Way of Praying Among Others

Among the various religions, Christianity has given rise to extremely varied forms of personal prayer, without designating any one as compulsory or necessary.

Rather, what is required is a balance between the various forms of prayer. If we were to take one way of praying, however venerable and recognised in the Christian tradition, and go on to make it the only way, it would be the same as selecting one aspect of the faith and making that the centre and exclusive focus of meditation. Such an approach will lead to an unbalanced spiritual life. The emotion one feels in front of the Christmas crib can bring about a deeper understanding of the meaning of the Incarnation, but it can also lead to childishness if it leaves no room for contemplation of the cross from time to time. And that in turn can lead to a spirituality marked by sadness if we ignore either the crib or the Resurrection. The

Christian life is a call to hold important things in balance, within which silent prayer can find its place.

It is always worth repeating that one of the distinguishing marks of Christianity, as distinct from other religions, is the extraordinary diversity of spiritual practices it has given rise to.

No one way of proceeding is superior to others. Too much attention to the steps taken toward a spiritual life can itself constitute a block. No one method, no one form of prayer, renders others useless or out of date. Each is a suggestion, a means, which will suit one person and not another, or be useful at one stage of life and then at another stage its usefulness wanes.

Silent prayer as presented here is therefore one form of prayer among others. It will appear to some to be just what they have been looking for, while others will find it too austere. This does not say anything about the quality of the spiritual life of one or the other, and even less about their progress on the spiritual journey. What matters is to be attentive to what each one needs at this point in time and that all are attentive to the foundational equilibrium of Christian prayer, the rhythm between speech and silence, between solitary prayer and community prayer, between contemplative prayer and intercessory prayer for the world.

How to Sit with God

THE WORD NEEDS SILENCE

For us humans, speech and silence are two related realities. No word is possible without silence: if everyone speaks at once, then we have confusion, not communication. For us, silence is always in relation to speech. When we become aware of the silence of a place or a moment, it is precisely because we know that noise or speech could have filled the place or the moment. Even alone in nature, we can make noise. We can even avoid silence by words (how many speak or sing on their own to camouflage the anguish of loneliness?)

There is therefore no need to revere either one or the other. The word is vital because we believe in a God who speaks, who creates the world by his Word and speaks to us by word. Silence, too, is needed to help us become more aware of God's transcendence. Words take us only so far and just because we have spoken about God does not mean we have fathomed the mystery. At the same time, words matter since it is by the handing on of a human word that God chose to make himself known.

If we take the risk of a more profound practice of silence, then our relationship to the word will be different. It will be less discursive and more restrained. For example, when we combine the prayer of intercession or petition with silent prayer, we no longer feel obliged to describe the situation to God in the smallest details, letting him know our story by telling it to him or explaining in detail all that he should do. We can content ourselves with naming those for whom we wish to pray, entrusting them to the blessing of God, or entering into prayer with them or in their name.

CHRISTIANS BELIEVE IN A GOD WHO SPEAKS

How we balance word and silence in Christian prayer tells a great deal about how we negotiate these two poles. We have to hold on to both sides. A taste for silence cannot dispense us from a faithful reading of the Word of God, just as the interest in the Bible must not transform the Christian into a tireless researcher, endlessly immersed in all kinds of commentaries.

Putting in place a fair balance between the received and meditated Word of God – the personal word addressed to God and the silence of God's presence – makes it easy to appreciate that these various forms of prayer are not in competition but rather enrich each other. Thus, for example, many find that their daily practice of silent prayer changes their way of reading or listening to a text, or their way of participating in the common worship. In silent prayer, they have learned to listen, which does not mean that they have heard anything, but that they know how to be available and attentive. By saying, or rather listening to the name which is at the heart of their prayer, they made themselves available to this simplest form of the Word of God: he is alive, and he bears a name and I can talk to him.

More concretely, one cannot recommend too strongly that in the time of personal prayer itself, each one should find his or her way of living this rhythm between speech and silence. When we pray in a group, it is quite possible to begin or end the time of silent prayer by reading a short text, a psalm or scripture verse, thus reminding ourselves that our prayer is always an answer to the Word of God, a response to the one who first called us by our name.

If more time is available, either every day or on days of rest, we can combine the practice of silent prayer with a form of meditation on the Word of God, such as the monastic *lectio divina*. The traditional practice of Christian monks is indeed a quiet reading of the Bible that develops in four stages: reading (*lectio*), understanding the text (*meditatio*), praying the text (*oratio*) and silent prayer (*contemplatio*). Some follow this traditional order; others, especially in active life, prefer to begin with the silent prayer that prepares them to receive the text, which helps them to make themselves available to the Word. Here, as always, what matters is not the scrupulous following of one method that we think of as effective, but rather what counts is the fidelity and the availability of the heart, supported by this or that practice.

SOLITUDE AND COMMUNITY

Once more, we find ourselves in the presence of two related realities. It is true that community prayer, in the liturgy or, more spontaneously, in the shared silence or in singing can be a great support for prayer and provide a significant experience of mutual support. But if we rely on the community to the point of never praying alone, then the community will not contribute anything. The community is not a boat or an aircraft carrier; it is the communion of those who pray. Solitary practice enriches community prayer and vice versa.

SOLITUDE AT THE HEART OF THE BODY OF CHRIST

Two Gospel texts speak to us of prayer, each emphasising one of the models. 'But whenever you pray, go into your room ... and pray to your Father who is in secret' (Mt 6:6). This is an invitation to solitary prayer, a moment of intimacy with God. 'For where two or three are gathered in my name, I am there among them' (Mt 18:20). This is a teaching about the real presence of Christ in his Church at prayer. It is not a question of having to choose one of these two texts so as to declare one form as the deeper and better. We must tirelessly find the means to connect the two forms, to live the solitude in communion with others, and to live in communion without losing sight of solitude. We are never outside the body of Christ, even in the solitude of our room, and we are never lost in the mass of believers, engaged in a collective movement that absorbs our personal relationship with God. As a member of the body of Christ, of the same nature as him and our brothers and sisters, we have for God a specific name that he alone knows. Cardinal Ratzinger underlined this dimension of prayer when he wrote:

The prayer of Jesus has been entrusted to the Church ('Pray then like this,' Lk 11:2). This is why when a Christian prays, even if he is alone, his prayer is in fact always within the framework of the 'Communion of Saints' in which and with which he prays, whether in a public and liturgical way or in a private manner.

Consequently, it must always be offered within the authentic spirit of the Church at prayer, and therefore under its guidance, which can sometimes take a concrete form in terms of a proven spiritual direction. The Christian, even when he is alone and prays in secret, is conscious that he always prays for the good of the Church in union with Christ, in the Holy Spirit and together with all the Saints.[1]

LEARNING TO PRAY

Today, in a culture that promotes individualism, we tend to privilege personal experience. Because the Christian experience is lived in the body of Christ which is the Church, the believer never ceases to live the relationship between his personal, unique path, and what he receives from his brothers and sisters in the faith. When our experience is not only spiritual but also lived in a religious way, we are nourished by roots which go really deep. The Christian tradition is above all a gathering up of experiences. The paths we travel do not have to be invented from scratch because other believers have walked them before us and found them to be good. They teach us a way of life and a way of praying. There is not one path: 'In my Father's house there are many dwelling places' (Jn 14:2). The life of the Church has developed various forms of prayer that all have their own uniqueness and coherence. Here again, we must remind ourselves that no one way of praying is the best, the deepest or the most Christian. To go to the school of tradition, to listen to the great spiritual masters, is not only to link with previous generations and to enter a centuries-old movement, but it is also a recognition that we have everything to learn.

SILENT PRAYER AND OTHER FORMS OF PRAYER

Among Catholics today we are witnessing a renewal of the practice of eucharistic adoration, especially among young people. Community prayer, in the form of vigils, before the Blessed Sacrament is offered as well as individual silent adoration. In the light of history, such a development is surprising, since adoration had emerged in times when believers rarely had permission to receive Holy Communion. In the absence of receiving, a spirituality of the presence and beholding of the consecrated host was offered to people instead. Today, however, those who participate in the Mass communicate easily and yet quite a number of them are touched by this practice of adoration. In particular, it often functions as an introduction to quiet prayer and to contemplative prayer.

Fundamentally, eucharistic adoration and the silent prayer presented here are not very different. In both cases, it is a question of standing in the presence of God, of contemplating his loving presence with us and of attempting to respond to it by our own presence.

These forms of prayer unfold in a climate that is more one of contemplation than of petition or reflection. Between the two, however, there is a subtle difference, but one that is important. It becomes apparent if one asks the seemingly simple question 'Where is God in prayer?' In sacramental adoration, we are facing each other: I am here and I look at the consecrated host, at the sacramental presence of Christ who is there, a few metres in front of me. This gives rise to the symbolism of making a visit, going to meet someone. In silent prayer, the emphasis is rather on what tradition calls 'indwelling', that is, the dwelling of God within us, his presence in the depths of the soul. The holy place is not before me, it is *in* me.

This can have quite practical consequences. Because of our attention to the presence of God in us, silent prayer can be done everywhere: at home, in a hospital room, on a journey, and so on. There would be some spiritual danger if someone were so attached to eucharistic adoration that it became the only valid form of prayer, seeing this as the only form of the real presence of God. 'Pray to your Father who is in secret.' This is done, according to the words of the Gospel, in one's room.

Silent prayer is therefore simpler, more accessible than adoration. It does not require going to a church or organising adoration with others. But this does not prevent anyone from making use of adoration from time to time, or being with other believers in the presence of the Blessed Sacrament by quietly saying the word of one's usual silent prayer.

THE PLACE OF PETITION AND INTERCESSION

An objection that is often made to contemplative prayer goes something like this. Is it not at heart a kind of selfish behaviour in which we do not care about others? Is intercessory prayer not an essential aspect of the Christian spiritual life? If contemplative prayer were lived as a moment of rupture with the rest of the world during which the believer would snuggle up in the arms of our Lord, taking no account of the human distress that surrounds us, it would indeed be open to valid criticism. This question must be kept in mind because such distortion is always possible. But there are several ways to establish a close connection between compassion and contemplative prayer. Silent prayer is not the only form of prayer: some people are used to distinguishing times of prayer devoted to intercession and other times to contemplative prayer, and this is already a way of responding to the question. But such a distinction in practice is not really satisfactory, for the one who prays in contemplative fashion is not cut off from the Church and the rest of humankind. In his own humanity, he stands in the presence of God, united, whether he likes it or not, with all the other beings who share this humanity, at the head of which stands Jesus Christ. Our prayer joins that of Christ. When someone prays, they pray in union with Jesus and his brothers and sisters, that's why we say *our* Father, not *my* Father.

When I am praying alone in my room, I am not really alone, because I am in union with the whole Church. Recollection and solitude are not a private affair. They only make sense as a communitarian act, that is to say, acts done by someone who knows themselves to be a member of a larger community of faith.

To pray for someone is not only to bring to God that person's suffering and to call God for help for that person. It can also be praying in someone's name. It is quite possible to live silent prayer in this spirit, standing in the presence of God in the name of those who do not pray, in the name of those who suffer, who may be named at the beginning of the time of prayer. With them, I sit in prayer. Such an approach can help us to remain faithful, because it is not only to heal my soul that I come back every day to this God-time, but also for them and in their name. My responsibility to them, to be precise, is to be steadfast in prayer, as Moses stood on the mountain with his hands raised while the people were fighting in the plain (Ex 17:8–16). In a paradoxical formula, Eckhart said: 'I will tell you how I think of people: I try to forget myself and everyone and merge myself, for them, in unity.'[2]

A CHRISTIAN PRACTICE CLOSE TO THE EAST?

This practice of silent prayer based on the repetition of a word has aspects in common with the spiritual practices of Eastern traditions. Some Christians even came to this type of prayer not by relying on the Christian tradition, but by seeking to import into Christianity what they first discovered in yoga or Zen.

But these personal journeys, to be respected as such, must not overshadow the extensive support that can be found for such a practice among Christian spiritual teachers from different periods. This tradition was long overlooked and this is no doubt why many Western Christians went to the East in search of teachings they did not find within Christianity. But this *break in tradition*, both in teaching transmission and in practice, should not be confused with an *absence of tradition*. Nor should it nourish the idea that this way of praying is exactly the same as non-Christian Eastern practices.

While the practical means, such as sitting in silence, do indeed resemble each other, the intention is radically different. In Christianity, there is no contemplation without dialogue: Christians are always listeners to the Word, which implies a relationship. In Zen, relationship is something that must be overcome; in Christianity, it is the heart of the spiritual life.

Rather than letting ourselves be beguiled by the East to the point of being either seduced or scared off, it is more interesting and more respectful of both Christianity and Zen or yoga to be cautious about reconciling or identifying aspects of either. Such efforts generally uncover a lack of knowledge. The name of God can be repeated without calling this practice a mantra, for it is not a mantra. One can read the Gospel without trying to understand it from the viewpoint of the Zen masters, because the Gospel text comes from a culture that has little in common with that of Zen. Inter-religious dialogue is difficult and demanding, and it requires a thorough knowledge of the religions that we are trying to engage in dialogue. To import casually into a Christian process one or another term from a radically different practice does not advance dialogue but rather feeds confusion.

It *is* possible to enter into dialogue with other religious traditions, to be fed by their teaching, up to a point, because there is a shared human wisdom, which is due to the fact that every human being is drawn to God. The Holy Spirit is at work in everyone and he speaks to the heart of believers in all kinds of ways. Christians do not have a monopoly on holiness. But they know whom they worship, and because of this they have nothing to fear from the possible resemblance of their practices to non-Christian practices. One day, at a session, a lady said to me anxiously, 'You are a priest and yet you sit in the lotus position!' If our attachment to Christ were to be endangered by a way of sitting, it would indeed be very fragile! There may be uses of certain postures or certain forms of mental repetition which aim at changes in the state of consciousness, so as to bring about a fusion of the human being with the cosmos, but that would hardly be compatible with Christian faith. But this is not a reason to prevent and even to forbid Christians a practice that might to some degree resemble that.

NOTES

1. Joseph Ratzinger, *Letter to the Bishops of the Catholic Church on some Aspects of Christian Meditation*, 15 October 1989, §7.

2. Meister Eckhart, *Sermons & Treatises*, Volume II, translated and edited by M. O'C. Walshe, Longmead: Element Books, 1979; Sermon 78, p. 226.

A Long History

In the *Catechism* of 1992, the Catholic Church encourages the practice of a way of praying based on the repetition of the name of Jesus:

> The invocation of the holy name of Jesus is the simplest way of praying always. When the holy name is repeated often by a humbly attentive heart, the prayer is not lost by heaping up empty phrases, but holds fast to the word and 'brings forth fruit with patience'. This prayer is possible 'at all times' because it is not one occupation among others but the only occupation: that of loving God, which animates and transfigures every action in Christ Jesus. (§ 2668)

The sobriety of this prayer (in which speech is reduced to one word) and the simplicity of its practice (which rests on the humble attention of the heart) have long attracted certain Christians. Wanting to devote time to God in a form as simple as possible and wishing to respond to the call of the Gospel by 'praying to their Father in secret' (Mt 6:6), monks and laity have sought to make themselves available and present to God. They understood that God is always close to us, present in the depths of our heart. In this perspective, prayer does not make God *present* but rather makes the person praying *attentive to the presence* of God.

It is difficult to give a date of birth to this way of praying. Already, in the Bible, a psalm proclaims:

> O Lord, my heart is not lifted up, my eyes are not raised too high; I do not occupy myself with things too great and too marvellous for me. I have calmed and quieted my soul, like a weaned child with its mother; my soul is like the weaned child that is with me. (Ps 131:1–2)

To hold one's soul in quiet and silence is certainly a fine definition of the inner attitude under discussion. We hold ourselves in that interior calm, so as to be available to the presence of God.

THE DESERT FATHERS

In the early Christian generations, from the third century onwards, men and women made the choice to go to the desert to lead a life of solitude in the presence of God. The Desert Fathers, the pioneers of Christian monastic life, have left a lasting mark on our history. Their teachings, the encouragement they gave each other when hermits had the opportunity to meet each other, have been preserved, in the form of short stories, the *Sayings of the Desert Fathers*. We see that their prayer consisted mainly of the Psalms. Most of them recited by heart the one hundred and fifty psalms each day.

Another important aspect of their spiritual struggle was the protection of the cell. Nothing is more tempting, when one is alone in the silence of the desert, than to seize all possible pretexts to go some other place, to visit a brother, or to go to town to do urgent shopping, in a word, to interact with the world. The monk in the desert, like every one of us today, sometimes had to fight with himself to remain present in prayer so as not to run away from it.

The earliest evidence for very short forms of prayer seems to come from these desert hermits. Such prayer was a kind of crying out to God with all their hearts.

Later, St Augustine mentions this as a venerable tradition coming from the desert.[1] These invocations were most often directed towards Christ and could consist of the saying of his name, calling for help or simply calling him to mind.

For some spiritual masters of the desert, this simple prayer had a physical component. They invite their disciples to sit in the silence of their cell: 'Sitting in your cell, be mindful of God.'[2] We even know that they used a kind of cushion, which also served as a pillow for the night.

CASSIAN AND PRAYER OF REPETITION

The art of monastic living was brought from the Christian East to the West in the fifth century, mainly through the *Conferences* of John Cassian, a text that was to become the basic manual of medieval spirituality. John Cassian travelled to discover the way of life of the Desert Fathers and subsequently he established monastic life in Provence. To convey what he himself had learned in the desert, he wrote, long after his journey, the *Conferences* which depicts the elders giving advice on the spiritual life. Regarding prayer, there is an echo of a repetitive prayer practice based on a biblical verse:

'O God, incline unto my aid; O Lord, make haste to help me.'[3] This verse should be poured out in unceasing prayer so that we may be delivered in adversity and preserved and not puffed up in prosperity. You should, I say, meditate constantly on this verse in your heart. You should not stop repeating it when you are doing any kind of work or performing some service or are on a journey.[4]

A similar verse from a psalm is recommended as the constant prayer of the monk, occupying his heart. This way of praying is based on repetition, and on filling the mind with the thought of God, but it is based on a verse and not on a word. The meaning of the repeated sentence is therefore important, as in the meditative reading of the Bible, *lectio divina*, to which this prayer is very close. In the same passage, Cassian in fact recommends the use of one verse for reflection throughout the day. The monk takes the sentence from scripture, either heard at prayer or read during his *lectio*. He keeps it in his heart and even on his lips throughout the day. This goes on until he gets to the heart of it and then he lets himself be touched by another sentence. In doing so, the monk prolongs his meditation of the text while he is no longer actually reading. He meditates, that is to say, he lets the message of the text resonate with him, with whatever feelings towards God the Word has aroused in his heart that day. And he changes the verse every day. It is important to be aware of both the closeness and differences of these various repeated prayers, not so much to compare them but to understand that they are not identical and that they lead to different spiritual approaches.

SAINT JOHN CLIMACUS AND SIMPLE PRAYER

Another major text of the monastic tradition is *The Ladder of Divine Ascent* of St John Climacus, which dates from the end of the seventh century. Here again, it is the wisdom of the Christian East which is transmitted. The book had a large influence in the West, because of the translations of this text first into Latin and then into French. John Climacus refers to a repetitive practice that makes it possible to reject thoughts that invade prayer.

He insists on being satisfied with a simple prayer, a sober word, to the point of reducing it down to a single word:

> In your prayers there is no need for high-flown words, for it is the simple and unsophisticated babblings of children that have more often won the heart of the

Father in heaven. Try not to talk excessively in your prayer, in case your mind is distracted by the search for words. One word from the publican sufficed to placate God, and a single utterance saved the thief. Talkative prayer frequently distracts the mind and deludes it whereas brevity (Greek: *monologia*) makes for concentration.[5]

Sobriety of speech in prayer has several functions.[6] The repetition of a simple word makes it possible to enter the prayer by fixing one's attention on the presence of God and by setting aside thoughts which are out of place. It allows the believer to hold himself in the presence of God over time, and prepares the soul to be taken up into silent union with God. We can see, then, that repetitive prayer is not only a psychological discipline, allowing us to focus our attention. Even more deeply, it discloses the movement of the heart towards God, that is the desire of our whole self to be in God.

THE PRAYER OF ONE WORD AND ORTHODOX MONKS

When we speak of the prayer of Eastern Christians, we are often tempted to identify it with the famous prayer of the heart, or prayer of Jesus, popularised by the Russian book, *The Way of the Pilgrim*. It consists of repeating tirelessly, throughout the day, the formula 'Lord Jesus, Son of the living God, have mercy on me, a sinner!' This is done in time with our breathing. This practice was developed in the monastic circles of Mount Athos in the fourteenth century. It is part of the long tradition[7] of hesychasm, a spiritual current that emphasised the simplicity of the monk whose sole effort consists in remaining calm, in staying peacefully in the presence of God, progressing in the knowledge of God in tandem with the knowledge of the self. In the same vein, we can find, in an earlier period, traces of a practice of repetitive prayer on the name of Jesus alone, called monologistic prayer, not in the sense of monologue, but in the sense of prayer using a single word. A contemporary Orthodox monk recalls the value of such a prayer:

Nevertheless, it should be remembered that the name of Jesus suffices of itself to constitute the prayer of Jesus. For the indefinition and fluidity which it had for many centuries, is substituted a determination quite rigid. But he who would like to return to primitive freedom and concentrate on the name alone, by abandoning the developed formula, would be entitled to say he practises the prayer of Jesus because he would bring back its ancient historical use.[8]

In this way, the literal meaning of one-word prayer – monologistic – becomes apparent because in this one word is the Word itself, spoken eternally by the Father.

Looked at this way, a new dimension of repetitive prayer opens up. When the repetition is not about a word, but about a name, about the name of the Lord, its austerity is a homage to the transcendence of the person to whom it is directed. When our prayer is too wordy it can disperse attention, but even more importantly, it does not take into account the fact that the one to whom the believer turns is the Word that the Father utters. The Father says the Word, and he says it in the soul, for he says it wherever God is present. By also saying the Word, the name of the Son, the believer enters, with humility and respect, into this movement of love of the Holy Trinity. The believer says only one word, but this word is the name of the one whose mystery exceeds all that the human being can say. This name refers to the Saviour without trying to define who he is or how he acts.

An heir to this tradition, Theoleptos of Philadelphia, who lived in the fourteenth century, teaches how prayer on the Lord's name feeds the knowledge of God:

> Prayer is the mind's dialogue with God, in which words or petition are uttered with the intellect riveted wholly on God. For when the mind unceasingly repeats the name of the Lord and the intellect gives its full attention to the invocation of the divine name, the light of the knowledge of God overshadows the entire soul like a luminous cloud.[9]

THE RHINELAND MYSTICS AND DETACHMENT

Let us now return to the West, to the banks of the Rhine at the same period. At the turn of the thirteenth and fourteenth centuries, Eckhart and his brothers did not teach a method of prayer. However, it is clear that their preaching called forth a form of contemplative prayer in which one seeks primarily to make oneself present to God, grounded in faith in God's presence within the human being and even more in the depths of the soul. The Rhineland spirituality is mainly about making the effort to be there. 'God is always ready, but we are unready. God is near to us, but we are far from him. God is in, but we are out. God is at home (in us), but we are abroad.'[10]

God, always present, is waiting for our soul to be available to him, free from all that encumbers us, free from everything that takes the place of God. 'It is very good when friend stands by friend. God stands by us, and remains standing by us, constant and unmoved.'[11]

This mutual presence of God to the soul and of the soul to God takes place in silence, a silence not wordless but beyond words. Eckhart recommends sitting quietly and letting God work and speak. This does not mean that we hear voices, because God works in the soul without our being able to say how it takes place.

THE CLOUD OF UNKNOWING

In England, again in the fourteenth century, an anonymous author, probably a Carthusian, wrote a little treatise on the life of prayer, called *The Cloud of Unknowing*, which had a considerable impact. It describes a form of Christian spirituality in which the believer is constantly moving towards God, because God is always beyond what we can know of him. The author gives practical advice, recommends turning one's heart towards God in prayer with the support of a little word tirelessly repeated. The function of the word here is mainly that of a shield against distractions. It is thanks to this word that the one who prays can take up the challenge again of turning his attention to God, without ending up in long speeches in which he could lose himself and forget how much the mystery of God goes beyond human words:

> So when you feel by the grace of God that he is calling you to this work, and you intend to respond, lift your heart to God with humble love. And really mean God himself who created you, and bought you, and graciously called you to this state of life. And think no other thought of him. It all depends on your desire. A naked intention directed to God, and himself alone, is wholly sufficient. If you want this intention summed up in a word, to retain it more easily, take a short word, preferably of one syllable, to do so. The shorter the word the better, being more like the working of the Spirit. A word like 'God' or 'love'. Choose which you like, or perhaps some other, so long as it is of one syllable. And fix this word fast to you heart, so that it is always there come what may.[12]

Our human words cannot contain the mystery of God and yet we need words to speak to God in prayer. It is better, therefore, to reduce our speech to its simplest and shortest form; the shorter the better. The author of the *Cloud* recommends that we keep our whole self in this word, without asking any question about its meaning, but using it to direct our entire being to God.

SAINT FRANCIS DE SALES AND SILENT PRAYER

In St Francis de Sales' letter written in 1604, we find advice that is very close to our subject. He had observed 'mental contortions' in the prayer of Mother Angélique Arnauld, abbess of Port-Royal. His advice to her was to dismiss useless thoughts by means of a repeated phrase:

> My daughter, a small, simple saying of some word from the Cross will drive away these thoughts or at least reduce their nuisance: 'O Lord, forgive this child of the old Adam, because she does not know what she does.' You should sing this very gently: 'He turns the mighty from their throne and he raises the humble.' It is better to make these rejections very slowly and simply and as if we were saying them for love and not because of a struggle.[13]

The proposed method is a little different from the repetition of a single word in contemplative mode. All the same, we may take from this witness, not only the fact that we find repetitive prayer in Francis de Sales, but also the excellent advice he gives at the end.

Repetitive prayer, if it is experienced as a struggle, in which the word or phrase is used as a weapon to silence temptations or distractions, is not likely to produce fruits of peace and contemplation. Certainly, we can always repeat the same word or phrase, but it should be due to love and not on account of stress. The word is very useful for 'making rejections' in order to keep unwelcome thoughts at bay, but we must reject them calmly, without nervousness and without excessive tension, by repeating, or rather by muttering, the word, like a confidence and even like a word of love. The essential is not the rejection, but the orientation of the heart towards God in love. This concise counsel, simply adapted to the practice of the prayer, is nevertheless of a great depth: in an understated way, it summarises an essential aspect of the spiritual combat which ought not to be felt as a struggle *against* evil, but rather a struggle *for* God.

Although he himself was attracted to highly structured prayer forms, including even meditation on single aspects of the faith, in his correspondence with Jeanne de Chantal, Francis de Sales emerges as a supporter of the simple prayer of presence. An echo of this spiritual dialogue is found in a conversation that was transcribed by the Sisters of the Visitation.

Saint Jeanne de Chantal:

> Should not the soul, especially in prayer, try to stop all kinds of discourse, effort, responses, curiosity and the like, and, instead of looking at what it has done or will do or is doing, the soul should look steadily towards God. In this way, the mind is uncluttered and one empties oneself of all care for self, being content with simply looking towards God and our own nothingness. We abandon ourselves to his holy will and its consequences, so as to stay content and tranquil, avoiding acts of the intellect or the will. I also think that in the practice of the virtues and in the struggle with faults and failures, one must not move from that position. This is because Our Lord puts the necessary sentiments into the soul so as illuminate it perfectly. Once and for all I say, all discourses and the use of the imagination will not take you there. You will say to me: Why are you leaving all that behind? O God, it is my misfortune and in spite of myself,

because experience has taught me that words and pictures can be harmful. But I am not mistress of my mind, which, without my permission, wants to see everything and more. That is why I ask my dear Lord for the help of holy obedience to put a stop to this unfortunate bumble bee, who is so afraid of absolute demands.

Saint Francis de Sales:

Our Lord, so long ago, has drawn you to this kind of prayer. He has allowed you to taste the desirable fruits which come from it and has shown you the futility of other methods.

Remain firm, then, and with the greatest gentleness you will be able to bring your mind back to this oneness and simplicity of presence and abandonment in God. And since your spirit would like to appeal to obedience, I say to it: My dear spirit, why do you want to pay the part of Martha in prayer, seeing that God has let you know he wants you to play the part of Mary? I command you, therefore, that you simply remain in God or near God, without trying to do anything about it, and without inquiring of him about anything, except as he prompts you. Do not rely on yourself, but rather be near to him.[14]

In another piece of advice given to Jeanne de Chantal, which deserves to be quoted here in its entirety, Francis de Sales gives a very concise description of this form of prayer:

> This simple loving trust and loving falling asleep with your spirit in the arms of the Saviour is an excellent understanding of all that you seek so earnestly. Remain in quiet resignation and surrender of yourself into the hands of Our Lord, without, however, forgetting to cooperate courageously and diligently with his holy grace by the exercise of the virtues and opportunities that will arise. Remain with Our Lord in this simple and pure child-like trust, without being concerned in any way about feelings or actions or understanding or the will.
>
> Remain there in peace, in a spirit of very simple and loving trust. And this attitude is not limited to prayer, where it is necessary to go with a great sweetness of mind, without any intention of doing anything else whatsoever, but only to be in the sight

of God in this simple surrender and rest in him, as he pleases. It is enough to content oneself with being in his presence, without seeing him or feeling anything or knowing how to imagine him. Do not ask anything of him, unless he encourages you to do so. Do not go back into yourself, but be there near to him. Such great simplicity is necessary not only in prayer but also in the way you live your life, setting aside and abandoning your whole soul, your actions, your successes, your business to the pleasure of God and at the mercy of his care. Keep firmly to this path.[15]

PRAYER IN SEVENTEENTH CENTURY FRANCE

Writing on prayer is really well developed during this century, which was century *par excellence* of mysticism in France. Many authors offered manuals, methods, some inspired by St Ignatius or by the authors of the Carmelite tradition. In the midst of this profusion of various practices, we find a stripped-down form of prayer, which some authors call 'the prayer of a simple regard'[16] and others 'the prayer of inner silence'[17] or 'prayer of the present moment'.[18] Though the title changes, the way of doing things is fairly constant. It is a question of emphasising one's presence to God, in a prayer that does not seek to elaborate a conversation of petition, thanksgiving or praise but to unify and simplify all the energy of the soul towards God. For example, the English Benedictine Augustine Baker, who lived in France in the first half of the seventeenth century, described the prayer of inner silence in this way:

> ... that she (the soul) with a silent attention regards God only, rejecting all manner of images of all objects whatsoever, and with the will she frames no particular request nor any express acts towards God, but remains in an entire silence both of tongue and thoughts ... with a sweet tacit consent of love in the will permitting God to take an entire possession of the soul as of a temple wholly belonging to him and consecrated to him, in which he is already present.[19]

Some authors recommend the rhythm of breathing to support this desire while others underline the posture.[20] Their teaching comes down to respect and propriety: to pray, it is necessary to take the proper position, and to be respectful of God in whose presence one is.

A COMMON PRAYER PRACTICE FOR ENGLISH MONKS
The writings of Dom Augustin Baker have always
been in print and they have nourished in the
monastic milieu of the English language a practice of
contemplative prayer. The letters of Dom Chapman,
several times quoted in this work, constitute a
particularly significant witness. These are letters in
which he directs the practice of silent prayer among
dialogue partners who are not monks, illustrating the
spread of this practice.

In more recent times, there has been a renewal of
this form of prayer among English-speaking monks
based on Eastern practices. John Main, after learning
meditation from a spiritual master, Swami Satyananda,
while working in Kuala Lumpur, Malaysia, became
a Benedictine monk in England. The swami had
invited him to meditate according to a 'Christian
mantra,'[21] that is, to enter into the repetitive practice
of the mantra without departing from his Christian
roots. He spent the rest of his life teaching this form
of Christian meditation, especially in North America.
Aside from Cassian, in whom he found the repetition
prayer of a biblical verse, John Main does not seem
to have been well informed of the many other points
of support offered to him by the Western Christian

tradition. This led him to attach great importance to the teaching of the East.

Almost at the same time, the American abbot Thomas Keating,[22] along with some of his Trappist brothers, was attempting to meet the spiritual expectations of Thomas Merton's readers by developing a practical method of contemplative prayer, based on the teaching of the *Cloud of Unknowing*. Like John Main, he recommends the use of a word, but leaves more freedom in the choice of the word. He also insists on the necessary association of this form of silent prayer with the meditative reading of the Bible (*lectio divina*). These two authors, mainly addressing an American public, were led to deepen the psychological dimensions of this practice, and to highlight its proximity to oriental practices. In their own setting, they did not feel the need to underline the roots in the Christian tradition of prayer on a single word.

WE ARE THE HEIRS OF THIS TRADITION

These few examples from the Christian tradition are sufficient to show that in the search for a simple form of prayer, that allows us to be in the presence of God in silence, we don't have to create it from scratch.

Christians have walked this path before us, and for centuries our ancestors were trying to devise methods to respond to this spiritual need. This long and rich tradition, however, like many other aspects of the spiritual life, experienced a rupture in transmission from the beginning of the eighteenth century. As a result, the focus of the Christian life in the following century fell mainly on activity, whether missionary, educational or penitential. Even the monks were caught up in this need for activity, in this mystique of tireless work for the Lord. It is, therefore, not surprising that when the need arose, in the second half of the twentieth century, many Christians turned to the East for contemplative practices, being convinced that there was nothing to learn from the Christian tradition. The enormous effort made by this generation to find the springs of inner silence have indeed borne fruit. We are now in a position to reconnect with our spiritual patrimony and to make the thrilling discovery of how those who went before us in Christian faith practised silent prayer. At the same time, we need not overlook the fruits of recent contact with the East, particularly when it comes to the bodily dimensions of meditation.

NOTES

1. St Augustine, *Letter 130 to Proba*, 9–10.

2. Theoleptos of Philadelphia, †1320 'On Inner Work in Christ and the Monastic Profession': G.E.H. Palmer, Philip Sherrard, Kallistos Ware (eds), *The Philokalia: The Complete Text*, Volume IV, London: Faber and Faber, 1995, p. 181.

3. Psalm 70:1 (69:2).

4. John Cassian, *The Conferences*, translated and annotated by Boniface Ramsey OP, New York: Newman Press, 1997; Conference 10.X.13–14, p. 382.

5. John Climacus, *The Ladder of Divine Ascent*, translated by Colm Luibhéid and Norman Russel, London: SPCK, 1982; Step 28, p. 275. See earlier in Step 28: 'Pray in all simplicity. The publican and the prodigal son were reconciled to God by a single utterance.' Ibid. p. 275.

6. 'The beginning of prayer is the explosion of distractions from the very start by a single thought (Greek: *monologistos*); the middle state is the concentration on what is being said or thought; it conclusion is rapture in the Lord.' John Climacus, *The Ladder of Divine Ascent*, translated by Colm Luibhéid and Norman Russel, London: SPCK, 1982; Step 28, p. 276.

7. See for example Tomás Spidlik, 'L'hésychasme', in *La Spiritualité de l'Orient chrétien*, t. *II. La Prière*, Rome, Orientalia Christiana Analecta 230, 1983, p. 321–356.

8. Cited in Lev Gillet, *The Prayer of Jesus: Its Genesis, Development and Practice in the Byzantine-Slavic Religious Tradition*, New York: Desclée, 1967, p. 68.

9. Theoleptos of Philadelphia, †1320 'On Inner Work in Christ and the Monastic Profession': G.E.H. Palmer, Philip Sherrard, Kallistos Ware (eds), *The Philokalia: The Complete Text*, Volume IV, London: Faber and Faber, 1995, p. 181.

10. Meister Eckhart, *Sermons & Treatises,* Volume II, translated and edited by M. O'C. Walshe, Longmead: Element Books, 1979; Sermon 69, p. 169.

11. Meister Eckhart, *Sermons & Treatises,* Volume I, translated and edited by M. O'C. Walshe, Longmead: Element Books, 1979; Sermon 24b, p. 194.

12. *The Cloud of Unknowing and Other Works*, translated into modern English by Clifton Wolters, Middlesex: Penguin, 1978, p. 69.

13. Francis de Sales, Letter 1604 to Mother Angélique Arnauld, 4 February 1620. English version by the translator.

14. Francis de Sales, Opuscule XXVI, end of May and August/November 1616. English version by the translator.

15. Francis de Sales, Opuscule XXIV. Advice to mother Jeanne de Chantal (1615–1616), vol. XXVI, p. 277–278. English version by the translator.

16. See for example, François Guilloré, *Conférences spirituelles pour bien mourir à soi-même*, Paris, chez Étienne Michallet, premier imprimeur du Roy, rue S. Jacques à l'image S. Paul près la fontaine S. Séverin, MDCLXXXIX, Conférence V, p. 317–343.

17. The expression comes from Dom Augustine Baker. See below.

18. See for example: *Exercices spirituels des religieuses bénédictines de la Congrégation de Notre Dame du Calvaire, composés par le très révérend Père Joseph de Paris, capucin de sainte mémoire, leur fondateur*, 1671, à Paris, de l'imprimerie de la veuve Edme Martin, rue Saint-Jacques, au Soleil d'or, p. 331–380. For a recent edition of the same, see: Père Joseph [François Joseph Leclerc du Tremblay], *L'Exercice du moment présent*, texte présenté par Jean-Marie Gueullette, Paris: Arfuyen, 2006.

19. Augustine Baker, *Holy Wisdom or Directions for the Prayer of Contemplation*, London: Burns and Oates, 1876, p. 493. Treatise III, section III; chapter VII.5. The chapter on prayer of silence may be found in Treatise III, section III, ch. vii.

20. On this subject, see Jean-Marie Gueullette, 'Les postures dans l'oraison. L'enseignement de François Guilloré SJ (1615–1684)', *Christus* 213, janvier 2007; p. 84–94.

21. John Main, *Word into Silence,* London: Darton, Longman and Todd, 2003.

22. Thomas Keating, *Open Mind, Open Heart: The Contemplative Dimension of the Gospel*, New York: Continuum, 1992.

Appendix 1

Psalms
The liturgical numbering of the psalms is given in brackets.

Psalm 16:1–2 (15:1–2)

Protect me, O God, for in you I take refuge.
I say to the Lord, 'You are my Lord;
    I have no good apart from you.'

Psalm 16:7–9 (15:7–9)

I bless the Lord who gives me counsel;
    in the night also my heart instructs me.
I keep the Lord always before me;
    because he is at my right hand, I shall not
        be moved.

Therefore my heart is glad, and my soul rejoices;
my body also rests secure.

How to Sit with God

Psalm 23:1–4 (22:1–4)

The Lord is my shepherd, I shall not want.
    He makes me lie down in green pastures; he
leads me beside still waters;
    he restores my soul.
He leads me in right paths
    for his name's sake.

Even though I walk through the darkest valley,
    I fear no evil;
for you are with me;
    your rod and your staff –
    they comfort me.

Psalm 31:1–5 (30:2–6)

In you, O Lord, I seek refuge;
    do not let me ever be put to shame;
    in your righteousness deliver me.
Incline your ear to me;
    rescue me speedily.
Be a rock of refuge for me,
    a strong fortress to save me.

You are indeed my rock and my fortress;
    for your name's sake lead me and guide me, take

me out of the net that is hidden for me,
    for you are my refuge.
Into your hand I commit my spirit;
    you have redeemed me, O Lord, faithful God.

Psalm 40:1–2 (39:2–3)

I waited patiently for the Lord;
    he inclined to me and heard my cry.
He drew me up from the desolate pit,
    out of the miry bog,
and set my feet upon a rock,
    making my steps secure.

Psalm 42:1–2 (41:2–3)

As a deer longs for flowing streams,
    so my soul longs for you, O God.
My soul thirsts for God,
    for the living God.
When shall I come and behold
    the face of God?

Psalm 62:5–7 (61:6–8)

For God alone my soul waits in silence,
    for my hope is from him.

How to Sit with God

He alone is my rock and my salvation,
 my fortress; I shall not be shaken.
On God rests my deliverance and my honour;
 my mighty rock, my refuge is in God.

Psalm 63:1–8 (62:1–9)

O God, you are my God, I seek you,
 my soul thirsts for you;
my flesh faints for you,
  as in a dry and weary land where there is
   no water.
So I have looked upon you in the sanctuary,
 beholding your power and glory.
Because your steadfast love is better than life,
 my lips will praise you.
So I will bless you as long as I live;
 I will lift up my hands and call on your name.

My soul is satisfied as with a rich feast,
 and my mouth praises you with joyful lips when
I think of you on my bed,
  and meditate on you in the watches of the night;
  for you have been my help,
  and in the shadow of your wings I sing for joy.

My soul clings to you;
> your right hand upholds me.

Psalm 73:22–23 (72:22–23)

I was stupid and ignorant;
> I was like a brute beast toward you.
Nevertheless I am continually with you;
> you hold my right hand.

Psalm 116:1–9 (14:1–9)

I love the Lord, because he has heard
> my voice and my supplications.
Because he inclined his ear to me,
> therefore I will call on him as long as I live.
The snares of death encompassed me; the
> pangs of Sheol laid hold on me;
> I suffered distress and anguish.
Then I called on the name of the Lord:
> 'O Lord, I pray, save my life!'

Gracious is the Lord, and righteous;
> our God is merciful.
The Lord protects the simple;
> when I was brought low, he saved me.

How to Sit with God

Return, O my soul, to your rest,
for the Lord has dealt bountifully with you.

For you have delivered my soul from death,
my eyes from tears,
my feet from stumbling.
I walk before the Lord
in the land of the living.

Psalm 130:6–7a (129:6–7a)

My soul waits for the Lord
more than those who watch for the morning,
more than those who watch for the morning.
O Israel, hope in the Lord!

Psalm 131:1–3 (130:1–3)

O Lord, my heart is not lifted up,
my eyes are not raised too high;
I do not occupy myself with things
too great and too marvellous for me.
But I have calmed and quieted my soul,
like a weaned child with its mother;
my soul is like the weaned child that is with me.
O Israel, hope in the Lord
from this time on and forevermore.

Psalm 139:1–3 (138:1–3)

> O Lord, you have searched me and known me. You
> know when I sit down and when I rise up;
>
> > you discern my thoughts from far away.
>
> You search out my path and my lying down,
>
> > and are acquainted with all my ways.

The Gospel according to Matthew (6:6–8)

But whenever you pray, go into your room and shut the door and pray to your Father who is in secret; and your Father who sees in secret will reward you. When you are praying, do not heap up empty phrases as the Gentiles do; for they think that they will be heard because of their many words. Do not be like them, for your Father knows what you need before you ask him.

The Gospel according to John (14:5–7)

Thomas said to him, 'Lord, we do not know where you are going. How can we know the way?' Jesus said to him, 'I am the way, and the truth, and the life. No one comes to the Father except through me. If you know me, you will know my Father also. From now on you do know him and have seen him.'

The Gospel according to John (14:20–21)

Jesus said to his disciples: 'On that day you will know that I am in my Father, and you in me, and I in you. They who have my commandments and keep them are those who love me; and those who love me will be loved by my Father, and I will love them and reveal myself to them.'

The Gospel according to John (15:4–5)

Jesus said to his disciples: 'Abide in me as I abide in you. Just as the branch cannot bear fruit by itself unless it abides in the vine, neither can you unless you abide in me. I am the vine, you are the branches. Those who abide in me and I in them bear much fruit, because apart from me you can do nothing.'

The Gospel according to John (15:9–11)

Jesus said to his disciples: 'As the Father has loved me, so I have loved you; abide in my love. If you keep my commandments, you will abide in my love, just as I have kept my Father's commandments and abide in his love. I have said these things to you so that my joy may be in you, and that your joy may be complete.'

The Gospel according to John (17:20–22)

Jesus prayed: 'I ask not only on behalf of these, but also on behalf of those who will believe in me through their word, that they may all be one. As you, Father, are in me and I am in you, may they also be in us, so that the world may believe that you have sent me. The glory that you have given me I have given them, so that they may be one, as we are one.'

Appendix 2

HELPFUL READING

Anon, *The Cloud of Unknowing and Other Works*, translated into modern English by Clifton Wolters, Middlesex: Penguin, 1978.

A Carthusian, *The Call of Silent Love*, Collegeville, MN: Cistercian Publications, 1993.

Burrows, Ruth, *Guidelines for Mystical Prayer*, Mahwah, NJ: Paulist Press, 2017.

Dalrymple, John, *Simple Prayer*, London: Darton, Longman and Todd, 2010.

Main, John, *Word into Silence,* London: Darton, Longman and Todd, 2003.

Le Saux, Henri (Abhishiktananda), *Prayer*, Canterbury: Canterbury Press, 2011.

O'Rourke, Benignus, *Finding Your Hidden Treasure: The Way of Silent Prayer*, London: Darton, Longman and Todd, 2011.

Index of Authors

In the course of this book, we have cited many writers from the Christian tradition. Reading these brief extracts can also be a help for entering into prayer.

The Cloud of Unknowing (anonymous) 153, 163

Augustine (saint), 43, 56–57, 145

Dom Augustin Baker, 161–163

Dom John Chapman, 24, 56, 60, 64, 65, 76, 162

Denis the Carthusian, 77

Meister Eckhart, 45, 53–54, 70, 85, 86, 93, 112, 114, 121, 139, 152–153

Francis de Sales (saint), 23–24, 66, 73–74, 85, 89–90, 120, 156–160

John Cassian, 19, 146–147, 162

John Climacus, 148–149

William de Saint-Thierry, 58

François Guilloré, 38, 39, 87–88, 160

Thomas Keating, 45, 163

Dom Henri Le Saux, 95, 122

John Main, 162, 163

Dom Claude Martin, 83–84

Paul (saint), 18, 22, 51

Peter Chrysologus (saint), 22

Joseph Ratzinger, 81–82, 85, 115, 132–133

Richard Rolle, 26, 27

Thomas Aquinas (saint), 72

Theoleptos of Philadelphia, 21, 59, 146, 152

Vincent de Paul (saint), 85